FRONTIER

Forts, Forests, and Flintlocks

True Stories about
Settlers, Soldiers, Indians, and Outlaws
on the Pennsylvania Frontier

JOHN L. MOORE

SUNBURY
P R E S S

Mechanicsburg, Pennsylvania   USA

8/8/2018
R.T.S.

Published by Sunbury Press, Inc.
50 West Main Street
Mechanicsburg, Pennsylvania 17055

www.sunburypress.com

Although the people whose experiences are chronicled in this book are dead, their stories survive in letters, diaries, journals, official reports, depositions, interrogations, examinations, minutes, and memoirs. These sources are quoted liberally. An occasional ellipsis indicates where words or phrases have been omitted. Punctuation and spelling have been modernized.

For information about special discounts for bulk purchases, please contact Sunbury Press Orders Dept. at (855) 338-8359 or orders@sunburypress.com.

To request one of our authors for speaking engagements or book signings, please contact Sunbury Press Publicity Dept. at publicity@sunburypress.com.

ISBN: 978-1-62006-513-6 (Trade Paperback)
Library of Congress Control Number: 2014956359

FIRST SUNBURY PRESS EDITION: November 2014

Product of the United States of America
0 1 1 2 3 5 8 13 21 34 55

Set in Bookman Old Style
Designed by Lawrence Knorr
Cover by Lawrence Knorr
Cover Art "Quick Decision" by Andrew Knez, Jr.
Edited by Janice Rhayem

Continue the Enlightenment!

JOHN L. MOORE's

FRONTIER PENNSYLVANIA SERIES

Bows, Bullets, & Bears
Cannons, Cattle, & Campfires
Forts, Forests, & Flintlocks
Pioneers, Prisoners, & Peace Pipes
Rivers, Raiders, & Renegades
Settlers, Soldiers, & Scalps
Traders, Travelers, & Tomahawks
Warriors, Wampum, & Wolves

Author's Note on Quotations

I have taken a journalist's approach to writing about the people whose lives and experiences are chronicled in this book. Long dead, they nonetheless speak to us through the many letters, diaries, journals, official reports, depositions, interrogations, examinations, minutes, and memoirs that they left behind.

Whenever possible, I have presented the people I have written about in their own words. My intent is to allow the reader a sense of immediacy with historical figures who lived two or more centuries ago. To accomplish this, I have occasionally omitted phrases or sentences from quotations, and I have employed an ellipsis (…) to indicate where I have done so. In some instances, I have modernized punctuation; and in others, spelling has been modernized.

John L. Moore
Northumberland, PA
October 2014

Dedication

For William N. Hague, who has dedicated many years to helping people learn to speak in public.

Acknowledgments

Jane P. Moore, Thomas Brucia, and Robert B. Swift read various segments of the manuscript and suggested improvements.

Frontiersman Liked to Display a 'Well-Riddled Target'

Autumn 1755

For generations, local historians in the Juniata River Valley told how a feisty frontiersman named James Patterson liked to demonstrate his marksmanship for Indians who were passing by. To show them how skilled he was, he shot his flintlock rifle at a target that he had put up on his homestead.

Patterson had taken up residence along the Juniata during the early 1750s. His cabin stood at present-day Mexico, along a major east-west trail that Indians used when traveling between central and western Pennsylvania.

Patterson "kept a well-riddled target at quite a distance from his house, and whenever he saw Indians coming near, he would fire at the target and let them examine the spot where the bullet entered, which thus always seemed to be at the center," according to Andrew Banks, an early Juniata Valley educator.

Patterson's skill became legendary, and the Indians gave him a nickname—"The Big Shot."

Banks's account, of course, is oral rather than documented history, but people who knew Banks, who was born in 1767 and once taught school in a log building, said that he had a remarkable memory and could "recall names, dates and facts at pleasure."

In the fall of 1755, as Indians allied with the French soldiers along the Ohio River Valley began raiding Pennsylvania settlements along the Juniata and Susquehanna Rivers, Patterson quickly fortified his cabin and recruited men to help him defend the countryside against the hostiles.

Governor Robert H. Morris

In early December Patterson wrote to Edward Shippen, a prominent fur trader and colonial leader at Lancaster, about deteriorating conditions in the Juniata settlements. Shippen passed Patterson's concerns along to William Allen, the chief justice of the Province of Pennsylvania: "He (Patterson) has built a stockade fort and has twenty men with him, which has been the only means of protecting the settlers thereabouts and keeping them on their plantations, He is a courageous resolute fellow ... and he is resolved to stand his ground, if he can be encouraged with a few arms and some ammunition. He wants very much to know whether any handsome premium is offered for (Indian) scalps, because if there is he is very sure his force will soon be augmented."

Patterson was exceptional in his ability to protect his homestead. Many of the whites who lived in Pennsylvania's frontier regions were skilled as farmers, but not as hunters, woodsmen, and fighters. Unlike Patterson, they lacked both the weapons and the knowledge needed to defend themselves and their homesteads.

From the safety of his office in Philadelphia, Governor Robert H. Morris wrote to his counterparts in other colonies and reported how Indians had "laid waste the settlements at a place called Tulpehocken," which he said "was one of the best peopled and most fruitful parts of this province," and only about seventy miles northwest of his city. "The people, who are under no kind of discipline and mostly without arms, are flying before them and leaving the country to their mercy," Morris said.

Unless they wanted to hunt for deer or bears, the settlers who had moved into the colony's interior had not needed firearms. In founding Pennsylvania in the early 1680s, William Penn went out of his way to establish peaceful relations with the Indians who regarded the country as theirs, not his. Penn was so thorough, thoughtful, and effective in doing this that the colony had been free from Indian wars until the outbreak of the French and Indian War in 1754.

In mid-October of 1755 a war party of Delaware Indians from the Allegheny River attacked settlements along the Penns Creek, a tributary of the Susquehanna River. Other Indian raids followed swiftly, and soon the entire Pennsylvania frontier was aflame. By the end of October, many people had abandoned their settlements along the Blue Ridge Mountains southwest of Carlisle. At Shippensburg, for instance, "this town is full of people, they being all moving in with their families five or six families in a

James Burd

house," James Burd wrote to his father-in-law, Edward Shippen, on November 2.

"We are in a great want of arms and ammunition, but with what we have are determined to give the enemy as warm a reception as we can," Burd added.

The townspeople had begun to build a fort "and expect to be finished in fifteen days, in which we intend to throw all the women and children. It would be greatly encouraging could we have reason to expect assistance from Philadelphia, by private donation of swivels, a few great guns, small arms and

4

ammunition," Burd said. "We would send our own wagons for them."

On October 31 William Parsons, who later became a major in the Pennsylvania Regiment, happened upon a large group of men who had gathered at the foot of the Kittatinny Mountain near present-day Bethel. A surveyor based in Easton, Parsons knew that the Shamokin Path came through a pass before it descended the mountain and that war parties used the path when coming to the region on raids.

Many of the one hundred men in the group had firearms, but "I found one-half of them without any powder or lead. However, I advised them to go forward, and them that had no ammunition I advised to take axes, in order to make a breastwork of trees for their security at night," Parsons said.

Parsons told the men that when they had blocked the pass north of Bethel, some of them should move west along the ridge and fortify the next gap at Swatara. The men should "stay there two or three days, in order to oppose the enemy if they should attempt to come that way." Parsons advised the men that he would ride over to Tulpehocken and arrange for "powder and lead, and a sufficient quantity of bread to be sent immediately after them."

To be sure, the settlers climbed the hill after he rode off, "but they went no farther than to the top of the mountain, and there those that had ammunition spent most of it in shooting up into the air, and then returned back again, firing all the way," Parsons wrote in a report to colonial leaders at Philadelphia.

At York on November 5 George Stevenson reported, "Such as have arms hold themselves ready, but, alas, they are few in number. Forty men came here yesterday willing to defend, but had but three guns and no ammunition, and could get none here, therefore went home again."

"Guns and ammunition is very much wanted here," Conrad Weiser wrote from Heidelberg in Berks County on November 19.

5

Benjamin Franklin

In January 1756 Benjamin Franklin was in Northampton County preparing to lead a column of Pennsylvania soldiers into the mountains to fortify strategic passes north of Bethlehem. "Just before we left Bethlehem, eleven farmers, who had been driven from their plantations by the Indians, came to me requesting a supply of firearms, that they might go back and fetch off their cattle," Franklin reported. "I gave them each a gun with suitable ammunition."

A steady rain began as Franklin's men moved out, "and it continued raining all day," he said. By the time the troops stopped for the night and took shelter in a barn, "we were ... as wet as water could make us."

Writing years later in his autobiography, Franklin remarked, "It was well we were not attacked in our march, for our arms were of the most ordinary sort, and our men could not keep their gun locks dry."

Franklin said that the farmers hadn't been as fortunate. The Indians had met them along the road and killed ten of the eleven. "The one who escaped informed that his and his companions' guns would not go off, the priming being wet with the rain," Franklin said.

In early 1756 the colony organized an army and sent a battalion of soldiers led by Colonel William Clapham up the Susquehanna River with orders to build a fort at the river's confluence at present-day Sunbury.

When the battalion began its upriver march from Harris's Ferry, the officers were dissatisfied with the quality of the muskets that the colony had provided. "The arms ... are as bad as you can conceive them to be," Captain Joseph Shippen wrote on June 2, from the camp at McKee's Store along the Susquehanna. "The locks are of the lowest price and continually out of order, so that we shall be obliged to take (gunsmith) William Henry with us to repair them from time to time, though he has already taken a great deal of pains to rectify them, and bore and straighten the barrels."

Shippen said that the battalion had recently received "about one hundred and fifty excellent short light arms, ... and I think the (Pennsylvania) commissioners ought to send us up two hundred or three hundred more of the same sort, and then order us to throw our Philadelphia arms into the middle of Susquehanna."

7

Indian Attacks Prompted Frontier Homesteaders to Flee

December 1755

Indian war parties attacked the white settlements along the upper Delaware River Valley several times during late 1755. This was territory that Pennsylvania colonial officials had forced the Minisink Indians to leave in the aftermath of the Walking Purchase of 1737. These raids had a devastating impact on the settlers, most of whom were farmers with little experience in fighting Indians.

"The whole country from the Minisinks quite to Easton is deserted by the inhabitants, and ... the Indians are wasting and destroying all before them as fast as they can, running from plantation to plantation," a colonial official named William Peters wrote to Governor Robert H. Morris on December 14.

By mid-December 1755, the Pennsylvania colony had appointed commissioners to organize the defense of the border settlements. One of them was Benjamin Franklin.

The commissioners wanted to recruit a force of five hundred men to defend the frontier. "Mr. Hamilton, Mr. Franklin and Joseph Fox ... propose to set out next Thursday towards ye parts where ye Indians are committing those ravages, in order to spirit up the people to act vigorously against them, and then to proceed to ye building block houses all along ye borders ... They talk of going as far as Shamokin (present-day Sunbury) to build a fort there, and don't propose to return till they have in some measures guarded the whole frontier," Peters reported.

Hyndshaw's Fort stood at the northeast end of a line of Pennsylvania posts that stretched nearly 190 miles across the frontier, ending at Chambers's Fort at Chambersburg. A small structure built in January 1756, Hyndshaw's consisted of a log stockade erected around the house of a settler, James Hyndshaw. Located in Upper Smithfield Township, it stood a short distance south of present-day Bushkill, near where Bushkill Creek empties into the Delaware River.

Benjamin Franklin authorized a small force based at Hyndshaw's. "I have ... allowed thirty men to secure the Township of Upper Smithfield, and commissioned (John) Van Etten and (James) Hyndshaw as captain and lieutenant," Franklin wrote on January 14, 1756.

Two days earlier, Franklin had given written orders to Van Etten, directing him "to proceed immediately to raise a company of foot, consisting of thirty able men, including two sergeants, with which you are to protect the inhabitants of Upper Smithfield, assisting them while they thresh out and secure their corn, and scouting from time to time as you judge necessary." Among other things, the captain was required to keep a journal of his day-to-day transactions.

Franklin also ordered him to inform his recruits that they were authorized to scalp any and all hostile Indians they might kill. "Forty dollars will be allowed and paid by the government for each scalp of an Indian enemy so killed; the same being produced with proper attestations," Franklin said. In other words, to collect the bounty, a soldier had to submit suitable documentation along with each scalp.

Riding into the Moravian village of Bethlehem on January 14, Franklin encountered a distressing situation: "As we drew near this place we met a number of wagons, and many people moving off with their effects and families from the Irish settlement and Lehigh Township, being terrified by the defeat of (Captain William) Hays's company, and the burnings and murders committed in the township on New Year's Day. We found this place filled with refugees, the

9

workmen's shops and even cellars being crowded with women and children; and we learned that Lehigh Township is almost entirely abandoned by the inhabitants."

Conditions weren't any better in the Minisinks, the region along the Delaware River north of Easton. As a rule, Indian warriors made few raids during winter, but the winter of 1755-1756 became a dramatic exception. On December 11, for instance, word spread throughout the region that a war party had attacked Daniel Broadhead's homestead in present-day Stroudsburg. Broadhead's neighbors saw that "the barn ... was on fire and heard the guns a firing." The next day, two men—John McMichael and Henry Dysert—told William Parsons, a justice of the peace at Easton, "that they saw the barn of the said Broadhead's on fire about nine o'clock in the morning ... and that they heard shooting and crying at Broadhead's house almost the whole day." Prior to the attack, Broadhead had erected a stockade around his house. McMichael and Dysert told Parsons that by late afternoon, Broadhead's dwelling "was yet unburnt, being, as they supposed, defended by the people within it."

As it happened, the house survived the attack, but Indian raiders returned to the region six weeks later. This time the attack in the Minisinks directly affected the new captain. "Mr. Van Etten's own barn, barracks, and all his wheat, are likewise burnt, and three of his best horses ... carried off by the enemy," the *Pennsylvania Gazette* reported in its January 29 issue.

With his military commission in hand, Van Etten lost little time in organizing a company of rangers. Less than two weeks after Franklin commissioned him, his men engaged in a firefight with enemy warriors. Quoting a letter written at Easton on January 30, the *Pennsylvania Gazette* reported: "Last Friday a party of Captain John Van Etten's men fell in with a party of Indians in Upper Smithfield, and killed and scalped two of them, and have good reason to believe they

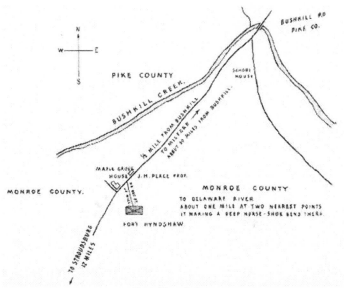

Fort Hyndshaw

wounded four or five more mortally. They got a booty of two guns, one of which a rifle, the other a smooth bored French gun; a fine pipe hatchet, and three match-coats. ... None of our people received any hurt."

In June 1756 Commissary James Young, who was paymaster for the Pennsylvania Regiment, toured many of the forts east of the Susquehanna River. Young gave Hyndshaw's Fort a positive review: "This fort is a square about seventy feet each way, very slightly stockaded. I gave some directions to alter the bastions, which at present are of very little use. It is clear all round for three hundred yards, and stand(s) on the banks of a large creek, and about one-quarter mile from the River Delaware, and I think in a very important place for the defense of this frontier."

As part of his visit, Young inspected the arms and ammunition available to the thirty-plus men stationed at Hyndshaw's. The provincial stores had only eleven "good muskets" and fourteen rounds of powder and lead for thirty men, four pounds of powder, and thirty

11

blankets, he reported. "Finding here such a small quantity of powder and lead, and this fort (located on) the most distant frontier, I wrote a letter to Captain (Jacob) Orndt at Fort Norris, where there is a large quantity, desiring he would deliver to this fort thirty pounds (of) powder, and ninety pounds (of) lead," Young said.

It had taken Young a full five hours to travel the fourteen miles from Fort Hamilton at present-day Stroudsburg to Hyndshaw's Fort, but the time included a brief stop at Samuel Dupui's fortified house at present-day Shawnee-on-Delaware. "Round Dupui's house is a large, but very slight, and ill-contrived stockade with a swivel gun mounted on each corner," Young wrote.

Hyndshaw's Fort was about nine miles north of Dupui's. "It is a good plain road from Dupui's, many plantations this way, but all deserted, and the houses chiefly burnt," he wrote.

Delaware Indian Chief Urges Runaway Slave to Organize Revolt

January 1756

Henry Hess, a nineteen-year-old illiterate farm boy, entered Pennsylvania history much against his will on New Year's Day 1756.

Along with his father Peter Hess and several other men, Henry was working on the Monroe County farm of his uncle, who was also known as Henry Hess, when at about 9:00 a.m. a war party of twenty-five Delaware Indians surprised them. The warriors killed two of the men, took Henry and his father as prisoners, stole three of the uncle's horses, and set fire to the stable.

A short time later, Henry watched as the Indians killed his father "in his presence, scalped him and took off all his clothes."

Then the warriors crossed a nearby mountain and caught up with five other Indians who had raided another settlement where they had taken two other prisoners, brothers Leonard, twenty, and William Weeser, seventeen, as they worked on their father's farm.

Months later, Henry Hess and Leonard Weeser gave detailed descriptions of their experiences.

Weeser: Before the war party left the settlements, "they burned the houses and a barrack of wheat, killed ye cattle and horses and sheep, and destroyed all they could." The warriors and the prisoners camped along the trail without any shelter.

Hess: "The Indians who were thirty in number in ye evening before it was dark, stopped and kindled a fire in the woods, first tying him and the two Weesers

13

with ropes and fastening them to a tree, in which manner they remained all night, though it was extremely cold, the coldest night as he thinks in this whole year.

"Some ... of the Indians were awake all night, it being as they said too cold to sleep. They seemed to be under no apprehensions of being pursued, for they set no watch."

Headed toward the Susquehanna River's North Branch, the war party traveled northwest through a dense pine forest known as the Great Swamp. The Indians took their captives to the Wyoming Valley, then went higher up the North Branch to Tioga at present-day Athens and later to other native settlements higher up the Susquehanna Valley in what is now New York State.

There were many white captives in these villages, and their captors often told them that once the Indians had owned all the land. "They said that all the country was their's, and they were never paid for it," Weeser reported later.

Hess made a similar report: "They would frequently say in their discourses all the country of Pennsylvania did belong to them, and the governors were always buying their land from them, but did not pay them for it."

In describing the January 1 raid, Weeser reported, "Among the Indians who made this attack and took him prisoner (was) Teedyuscung alias Gideon alias Honest John."

Born circa 1700 near Trenton, N.J., Teedyuscung was known as Honest John when he was a young man. He made and sold brooms to white settlers. He later moved to Pennsylvania. The Moravians at Bethlehem converted him to Christianity and baptized him as Gideon.

When the French and Indian War began in 1755, Teedyuscung went on the warpath, which led him to the Hess and Weeser farms, described as "plantations" by eighteenth century writers.

Teedyuscung alias Gideon alias Honest John

Weeser: "The Indians would frequently say in conversation they and the French would gather in a body together and come down to Pennsylvania and kill all the inhabitants, for it was their, meaning the Indians,' country, and they would have it again."

Hess: "Teedyuscung was frequently in conversation with a Negro man, a runaway, whose master lived somewhere above Samuel Dupui's (at Shawnee-on-Delaware), and he overheard Teedyuscung advising him to go among the inhabitants, and talk with the Negroes, and persuade them to kill their masters, which if they would do he would be in the woods ready to receive any Negroes (who) would murder their masters, and they might live well with the Indians."

There's no indication that such a slave revolt ever took place in Monroe County.

By autumn, Teedyuscung was more interested in making peace than war, and in October 1756 he released four captives including Hess and Weeser. The two subsequently gave detailed statements to Pennsylvania officials following their release. This narrative is based on their statements, which appear in a volume of colonial records known as the Pennsylvania Archives.

Ben Franklin Hired New England Soldier who Built Fort Augusta

February 1756

Chief Shikellamy was delighted when blacksmith Anton Schmidt came to live in the Indian town of Shamokin in 1747. Schmidt's presence meant that Indian hunters could get their guns repaired without traveling to the white settlements south of the Blue Ridge Mountains.

Shikellamy had asked the governor of Pennsylvania to send a smith to Shamokin, which was located at the confluence of the Susquehanna River's West and North Branches. The town occupied part of present-day Northumberland, Packers Island, and the northern part of modern Sunbury.

The Indians gave Schmidt deerskins and bearskins as payment for fixing their firearms. The blacksmith was part of the Moravian Church mission in Shamokin. Records of the mission show that native hunters also provided the blacksmith with a steady supply of fresh venison.

When Shikellamy died in 1748, the Moravians built a wooden coffin for him, and Schmidt was one of four men who carried the old chief in the coffin to his grave, according to J. F. Meginness, writing in *Otzinachson, a History of the West Branch Valley.*

Nine years later the missionaries fled from Shamokin when hostile Indians began attacking Pennsylvania's frontier settlements; that was during the French and Indian War.

In December 1755 the Moravian blacksmith traveled to Philadelphia to guide a small military force headed by Benjamin Franklin over muddy, country

Shikellamy

roads to Bethlehem, where the Moravian Church was based. Franklin's column included a wagon carrying firearms for settlers to use against enemy Indians, reported James B. Nolan, author of *General Benjamin Franklin: The Military Career of a Philosopher*. It also transported equipment for building stockade forts on the frontier.

Schmidt was one of four men involved in Franklin's march into the mountains north of Bethlehem and Easton who also had ties to Shamokin and Fort Augusta, which Pennsylvania soldiers built in 1756 to fortify the forks of the Susquehanna. The three others were Samuel Miles, Charles Beatty, and William Clapham.

Samuel Miles was a sixteen-year-old volunteer from Lancaster. His company was "ordered to Northampton County and rendezvoused at Easton under the command of General Dr. Benjamin Franklin," Miles said in his memoirs, which he wrote in 1802.

Franklin led the soldiers into the mountains along the Lehigh River. "We erected a fort there, to which was given the name Fort Allen," Miles wrote.

Ben Franklin, writing in his autobiography, said he was at the newly erected Fort Allen when a military man named William Clapham came to visit. It was late January 1756 or early February, and Franklin's soldiers had built four forts along the Northampton frontier. Franklin appointed Clapham—"a New England officer ... experienced in Indian war"—to lead Pennsylvania's military effort. The New Englander readily "consented to accept the command," and thus freed Franklin to return to Philadelphia.

Six months later, Clapham commanded the Pennsylvania Regiment's 3rd Battalion, which built Fort Augusta during the summer of 1756. Samuel Miles was one of his soldiers.

As Miles later wrote in his memoirs, "we marched for Shamokin, an Indian town, the inhabitants of which had been very troublesome to the frontier

19

Rev. Charles Beatty

settlements." The regiment came up the west side of the river, and when it reached present-day Shamokin Dam, the soldiers crossed the river in flat-bottom boats.

"I had the honor of being the first man who put his foot on shore at landing," Miles wrote.

The chaplain at Fort Augusta was the Rev. Charles Beatty, who had also accompanied Franklin in his trek up the Lehigh. In *The Autobiography of Benjamin Franklin*, Franklin reported that Beatty one day "complained to me that the men did not generally attend his prayers and exhortations."

Franklin suggested that the chaplain give the soldiers their daily ration of rum following worship services. The chaplain agreed, and "never were prayers more generally and more punctually attended," Franklin wrote.

When Colonel Clapham led his column up the Susquehanna in late spring, the clergyman considered it his duty to minister to the troops. Even so, there were times when he didn't like being in their company. One of them was July 4. "One of the bateaux which had on it a cannon was upset, which occasioned a great deal of labor, and what profane swearing was there," Beatty wrote in his journal. "If I stay in the camp, my ears are greeted with profane oaths, and if I go out to shun it, I am in danger of the enemy—what a dilemma is this?"

By late July, the soldiers had reached the site of Fort Augusta and had started construction. When the colonel ordered a detachment to attack an Indian town on the upper West Branch, the chaplain felt an obligation to go along. As he wrote on July 23, "this morning very early the scouts, which consisted of about 100 men, dressed like the Indians, some being blacked, others painted, crossed the river into the fork, in order to go toward the west, with ten days' provisions; thus by taking the Indians in their own way, hoped to be able to beat them in their turn."

The soldiers were less than enthusiastic when they learned that the clergyman wanted to go along. Beatty wrote that he "was grieved that they seemed to have little regard for the blessing of God, which alone can make them successful. Had an inclination to go with them, but they did not seem very desirous of it, and the colonel thought it best for me to stay, so I took this as a hint of Providence."

When the scouts headed up the West Branch, the chaplain remained at Fort Augusta.

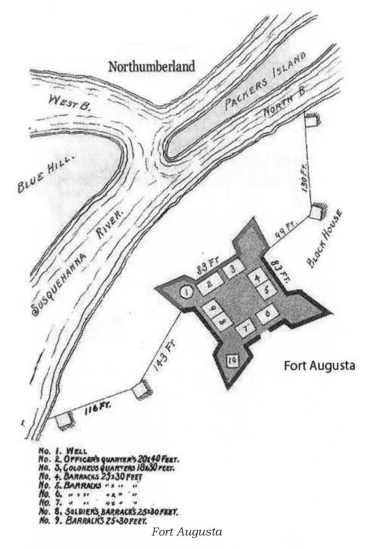

No. 1. WELL
No. 2. OFFICER'S QUARTERS 20x40 FEET.
No. 3. COLONEL'S QUARTERS 18x30 FEET.
No. 4. BARRACKS 25x30 FEET
No. 5. BARRACKS " x " "
No. 6. " " " " x " "
No. 7. " " " " x " "
No. 8. SOLDIER'S BARRACKS 25x30 FEET.
No. 9. BARRACKS 25x30 FEET.

Fort Augusta

How Skilled Were
Pennsylvania Shooters?

June 1756

Pennsylvania soldiers who fought Indians during the French and Indian War needed to be skilled marksmen. Were they? To shoot accurately, they had to have firearms of an acceptable quality. Did they?

Adequate data to measure the skills of the soldiers and to assess the quality of their guns doesn't exist, but entries in journals kept by two officers of the Pennsylvania Regiment shed a little light on the issue.

Commissary James Young was one of the two officers. In June 1756 he made an eight-day inspection tour of thirteen forts, fortified farmhouses, and other outposts between Reading and the Delaware River where Pennsylvania troops were stationed. The journey took Young over roughly 140 miles of frontier roads, and, as part of his inspection of each place, he took an inventory of equipment and supplies in the post storerooms. On occasion, he also had the men demonstrate their shooting skills.

Young's tour took place only eight months after Indian raids had begun in the colony's outlying regions. When the border war started, the province lacked both an army and the supplies necessary to provision and equip it. Moreover, few, if any, of the outposts Young inspected had even existed when Indians began attacking Pennsylvania settlements in October 1755.

The first shooting demonstration that Young conducted took place on June 21, 1756, at Fort Lebanon, near present-day Auburn in Schuylkill County. "I ordered the men to fire at a mark. Fifteen of twenty-eight hit within two foot of the center, at the

Colonial troops on patrol

distance of eighty yards," Young said. In other words, 54 percent of the soldiers hit the target, and 46 percent missed.

The commissary moved on to the fort near Allemangel, near modern Snyders, also in Schuylkill County, and early the next morning, "I ordered the people to fire at a mark," Young reported. "Not above four in twenty-five hit the tree at the distance of eighty-five yards." That's only 16 percent, with 84 percent of the soldiers missing the target completely.

On June 26 the troops posted in Easton displayed much better skills and had the best scores. "At 9 a.m. mustered the company stationed here," Young reported. "Found them stout, able men, their arms in good order. They fired at a mark, sixteen of twenty hit within nine inches of the center at eighty yards distance." That works out to an impressive 80 percent

24

and clearly reflects competent shooting skills and high-quality weapons.

Young's journal only includes these three instances of marksmanship tests.

Although Young reported that the troops posted at Easton had firearms of an acceptable quality, other provincial guns stored in the town were in much worse shape. Major William Parsons had charge of an armory in Easton with weapons "for the use of the inhabitants," Young said. He reported finding "thirty-seven bad muskets" and "a parcel of broken muskets." He didn't report finding any firearms in good condition.

At Reading, earlier in the tour, Young had found "twenty-five good muskets, twenty-five muskets in need to repair, and eleven broken ones." At Fort Norris there were thirteen good muskets, three "burst" ones, and "sixteen very bad," he wrote.

When Young inspected the stores at the Fort at North Kill, near present-day Shartlesville, he found eight good muskets, but only four rounds of powder and lead per man. "I inquired the reason there was so little powder and lead here. The sergeant told me he had repeatedly requested more of Captain (Jacob) Morgan, (his superior at nearby Fort Lebanon), but to no purpose," Young wrote.

Sixteen months later, in February 1758, Colonel James Burd made a seventeen-day, 150-mile inspection tour of the colony's forts between Fort Hunter on the Susquehanna River and Hyndshaw's Fort on the Delaware River.

Burd found eighty soldiers stationed at Fort Hunter, and "the captain informs me that they have not above three loads of ammunition a man," the colonel wrote on February 18. He promptly dispatched a rider with orders "to send up here a barrel of powder and lead" from another post that had enough ammunition to share.

At Fort Swatara, near present-day Lickdale in Lebanon County, an inspection of the storeroom on

February 21 determined that there were "no province arms fit for use," Burd said. Before he moved on, he told the officers that he wanted "a target to be erected six inches thick, in order to practice the soldiers in shooting."

Fifty miles to the east at Fort William, near present-day Auburn, the colonel reported on February 25 that he "found fifty-three good men, but deficient in discipline." The question of firearms was another matter altogether. Although the men were equipped with muskets, the fort's storeroom contained three quarter casks of powder, 150 pounds of lead, and 400 flints, but "no arms fit for use," Burd wrote.

The colonel had the men demonstrate their prowess in shooting. "Here I found a target erected, (and) ordered the company to shoot at the mark," he said. But first he "set them the example myself by wheeling round and firing by the word of command. I shot a bullet into the center of the mark the size of a dollar, distance one hundred yards."

As for the soldiers, "some of them shot tolerable bad," the colonel said. "Most of their arms are very bad." Burd's report didn't include any statistics.

At Fort Allen in present-day Weissport on February 28, Burd said that he "ordered Captain (Jacob) Orndt … to put up a target six inches thick to learn the soldiers to shoot." There was plenty of ammunition in the fort's storeroom—two hundred-twenty-five pounds of gun powder, three hundred pounds of lead, and five hundred gunflints. In terms of weapons, Burd noted the presence of two swivel guns without referring to their condition, and twenty-six muskets that he rated as "bad."

Flintlock Muskets Versus Rifled Guns

April 1756

When a man shouldered a gun to fire at a foe on the Pennsylvania frontier during the 1750s, his weapon was either a musket or a rifle.

An experienced fur trader, Edward Shippen expressed a strong preference for what he called "rifled guns" over smooth-bored muskets.

Writing to Governor Robert H. Morris on April 24, 1756, from Lancaster, where he was a prosperous merchant, Shippen said, "I cannot say I have been pleased with ye sight of any of the guns which have been carried through this borough for the service of the province."

He explained in concise detail:

"The Indians make use of rifled guns for the most part, and there is such a difference between these sort of guns and smooth-bored, that if I was in an engagement with the savages, I would rather stand my chance with one of the former sort, which might require a minute to clean, load and discharge, than be possessed with a smooth-bored gun which I could discharge three times in ye same space, for at a hundred and fifty yards distance, with the one, I can put a ball within a foot or six Inches of ye mark, whereas with the other, I can seldom or ever hit the board of two feet wide and six feet long."

In other words, a rifled gun, or rifle, had a greater range and provided greater accuracy than a musket did.

There were similarities but also important differences between the two types of gun.

To begin with, the similarities: each was loaded from the muzzle, or business end, of the gun barrel, and each relied on a mechanism called a flintlock to discharge black powder and projectile that had been loaded in the barrel by means of a ramrod.

Here's how the firearm worked: The flintlock consisted of a metal device, called a cock, that held a piece of flint. Pulling the trigger propelled the cock forward so that the flint struck a metal piece called a frizzen. This created a spark that ignited a small

Edward Shippen

quantity of gunpowder contained in a small, metal pan situated outside of and alongside the rear of the barrel. The resulting flash of fire traveled through a small opening, or touchhole, in the barrel that led to the weapon's firing chamber. This ignited the main charge of gunpowder, and the resulting explosion expelled the projectile out of the barrel with tremendous force at a very high speed.

The inside, or bore, of the barrel of a musket was smooth. This gun was often used to fire lead balls.

In contrast, the bore of a rifle had a groove that spiraled along the entire length of the barrel. The groove caused the bullet to spin. A bullet fired by a rifled gun went farther and with greater accuracy than did a ball shot from a musket.

As Shippen indicated, it took longer to clean and reload a rifle than it did to reload a musket.

It's easy to understand why Shippen had observed that Indians had a marked preference for rifles. During hunting season, most Indian men spent a good deal of their time in pursuit of game. They needed meat to feed their families and skins to sell to white traders. Native hunters were free to kill as many animals as they wanted or needed, and this created intense competition for game. They quickly came to realize that the degree of their success depended on the accuracy and reach of their firearms. In short, they couldn't afford to miss a shot. They quickly saw the advantage in hunting with rifled guns.

By the time the French and Indian War reached the Pennsylvania settlements in October 1755, Indian men had already become skilled marksmen who chose rifles over muskets. In contrast, soldiers who joined the Pennsylvania Regiment in 1756 were issued muskets rather than rifles. When James Young, the regiment's commissary general, made a tour of provincial forts between Reading and the Delaware River in June 1756, he found stores of muskets, but no rifles, at each outpost. Two years later, in May 1758, Captain Harry Gordon, a British military engineer, recommended that six hundred muskets (complete with cartridge boxes, brushes, and priming wire), sixteen hundred gun flints, twenty-five thousand musket balls, and one hundred and twenty barrels of gun powder be shipped to Fort Augusta. Gordon's report made no mention of rifled guns.

Conrad Weiser, in describing an incident that happened in eastern Pennsylvania on November 21, 1756, remarked while visiting Easton, "a certain Indian, called Armstrong, had a rifled gun taken or stolen from him. ... When we came to Fort Allen, this Indian demanded a rifled gun of me. ... I offered him one of the Provincial spare guns, but he did not like it and gave it back. ... so ... I bought a German gun from one of the soldiers for thirty-five shillings and gave it to the Indian, which satisfied him, and I paid for the gun."

This anecdote makes a good point. Fort Allen was one of the forts that Young had inspected five months earlier, and the provincial gun that Weiser mentioned in all likelihood was a musket.

Delaware War Chief: 'I Can Take any Fort that Can Catch Fire'

July 1756

In late 1755 and early 1756, as Pennsylvania hurriedly organized an army to defend against Indian attacks, the colonial leaders often accepted men with little or no military training or experience as soldiers and officers. The log forts that these recruits erected as defensive outposts across the frontier occasionally reflected this fact.

To be sure, some officers in the new Pennsylvania Regiment built sturdy structures capable of withstanding attack, but others erected forts that lacked wells inside the stockade or had other serious flaws. The reports of two senior officers, who in June 1756 inspected posts garrisoned by the Pennsylvania Regiment, reveal the seriousness of this slipshod construction.

After visiting Fort Lebanon (present-day Auburn) on June 3, Major William Parsons gave a scathing report of conditions there.

"The palisades of the fort in many places stand so far from one another, that (it) is as safe for an enemy without to fire into, as it is for the garrison to fire out of it," he said. Also, the upright logs in the stockade walls were so loose in the ground that "in some places I am persuaded I could have thrown down the palisades with my hands without the help of any tool."

When Commissary James Young reached the Fort at North Kill (present-day Shartlesville) on June 20, he saw that the post had been built "in a very thick wood on a small rising ground." The clearing in which the fort stood was less than one hundred yards across, and Young realized that hostile Indians could hide behind trees at the edge of the clearing and shoot into it. "The woods are not cleared above forty yards from the fort," he noted. To remedy this, "I gave orders to cut all (trees) down for two hundred yards."

There was a second major issue: "The stockades are very ill fixed in the ground, and open in many places." Clearly, the soldiers needed to install additional palisades to close the gaps.

Four days later, Young was equally displeased when he inspected Fort Hamilton (present-day Stroudsburg) on June 24. The fort had been built in the shape of a square "with four half bastions all very ill contrived and finished. The stockades (were) open six inches in many places, and not firm in the ground, and may be easily pulled down."

Fort Hamilton had one gate, and the soldiers had erected some log palisades outside of the gate as a cover. Young realized that during an attack these logs could well serve as "a great shelter to an enemy. I therefore ordered to pull them down. I also ordered (the garrison) to fill up the other stockades where open."

Fort Shirley occupied a hill along Aughwick Creek (present-day Shirleysburg) about five miles south of the creek's confluence with the Juniata River. In erecting the post, the workers hadn't bothered with digging a well. Instead, they relied on the stream, which ran "at the foot of a high bank" on the fort's east side, according to Colonel John Armstrong. Consequently, "Fort Shirley is not easily defended, and their water may be taken possession of by the enemy," Armstrong said.

There was another type of flaw at Fort Granville, which sat along the Juniata River at present-day Lewistown a short distance to the west of a mountain pass. Governor Robert H. Morris thought the post had an excellent location. "This fort commands a narrow pass where the Juniata falls through the mountains which is so circumstanced that a few men can

John Armstrong

maintain it against a much greater number, as the rocks are very high on each side." The Juniata Path, a well-used, east-west Indian trail, also went through this pass.

Like other Pennsylvania outposts, Fort Granville was constructed of logs. To build it, the soldiers cut logs into sixteen-foot lengths. The logs were then placed upright in narrow trenches about four feet deep. The log walls formed a square, and bastions were built at each corner. The fort had one gate.

Curiously, the officers that selected the site for Fort Granville placed it quite close to a small ravine

33

that cut through the river bank and led directly to the Juniata. The men in the garrison could have graded the top and side of the gully, but Captain Edward Ward—and his predecessor, Captain James Burd—had neglected to do this. In the end, this omission proved to have fatal consequences.

Around nine o'clock on the morning of July 30, Ward took most of the soldiers in his command and marched off to the Shermans Valley some thirty-five miles to the southeast. Farmers there were reaping their mid-summer crops and Ward's men were needed to guard them. Ward's departure left Lieutenant Edward Armstrong in command with a force of twenty-four men.

Ward's column had been gone about two hours when Delaware Indians led by Captain Jacobs and a detachment of French soldiers showed up. Armstrong's men traded shots with the enemy, who numbered about fifty-five. The shooting continued back and forth until evening. By this time, the attackers realized that by following the river bank a short distance above the fort, they could reach the ravine and get within forty feet of the stockade. The side of the ravine sheltered them from any gunfire from inside Fort Granville.

The Indians and French soldiers gathered pine knots and other combustibles and carried them into the gully under cover of darkness. Protected by the side of the ravine, the warriors tossed the wood "against the fort, till they made a pile and train from the fort to the gut, to which they set fire, and by that means the logs of the stockade catched (fire), and a hole was made, through which the lieutenant and a soldier were shot, and three others wounded, while they were endeavoring to extinguish the flames," according to a Pennsylvania soldier named Barnhold.

Another soldier of the garrison, Peter Walker, later reported that by the second day of the siege, the garrison didn't have any drinking water and that the Indians and French had often called on the lieutenant to surrender. The fighting continued, and Lieutenant

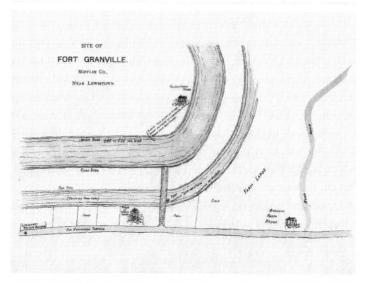

Armstrong shot a French soldier who "was erecting his body out of the hollow to throw pine knots on the fire made against the fort," Walker said.

Eventually, the lieutenant's wound proved fatal. With Armstrong dead, command passed to Corporal John Turner. According to the August 19 edition of the *Pennsylvania Gazette*, "The enemy then called to the besieged and told them they should have quarter, if they would surrender ... John Turner immediately opened the gates, and they took possession of the fort. ... They made prisoners (of) twenty-two soldiers, three women, and five or six children, of which the French took the young men and women, and the Indians the older men and children. ... Having loaded them with flour, etc. they set off, after setting up French colors near the fort ..."

According to Peter Walker, as the Indians came into the fort, a soldier named Brandon, "who had been shot through the knee ... called out, 'I am a Roman Catholic and will go with you,'" but the Indians, "observing he could not march, soon dispatched him with a tomahawk."

35

Walker and Barnhold were among the prisoners. As the French and Indians led the captives away, Captain Jacobs torched the fort. Walker reported that Jacobs boasted later that "he could take any fort that would catch fire." The chief also expressed willingness to eventually make peace with the English, but only "when they had learned him to make gunpowder."

News of the fort's fall spread quickly across Pennsylvania. Influential leaders from Cumberland County told Governor William Denny that "there never was in the memory of man a more abundant harvest," but "after the burning of Fort Granville ... the farmers abandoned their plantations and left what corn was not then stacked or carried into barns to perish on the ground." These men argued that the situation had become so extreme that unless the colony significantly strengthened its military operations in the region, "the west side of Susquehanna would be entirely abandoned."

As for the corporal who had surrendered the fort, the *Pennsylvania Gazette* eventually reported that the Indians burned him at the stake at the Delaware town of Kittanning on the Allegheny River. "They tied him to a black post, danced round him, made a great fire, and having heated gun-barrels red hot, they run them through his body," according to I. D. Rupp, whose 1847 history of Mifflin County included a detailed account of the fall of Fort Granville. After torturing Turner for three hours, the Delawares scalped him and finally "held up a boy with a hatchet in his hand to give him the finishing stroke."

Settlers Offer Armed Resistance

November 1756

Sunday evening on November 28, 1756, a number of settlers had gathered at the Schlosser cabin located south of the Blue Mountain in eastern Pennsylvania. As twilight gave way to darkness, they went inside and closed—and probably barred—the door. One of the settlers, possibly Schlosser, had a gun.

His homestead was located in a region called Allemangel, which today lies partly in Lynn Township in western Lehigh County and partly in Albany Township in eastern Berks County.

Suddenly there was a knock on the door. As John Holder told Timothy Horsfield, the justice of the peace at Bethlehem, two days later:

"The people within called, 'Who is there?' Answer was made, 'A good friend.' They within not opening the door, they knocked again. They within answered, 'Who is there?' No answer being made from without, then one of the men, named Stonebrook, looked out of the window. ... An Indian discharged a gun and killed him on the spot. They then opened the door, the woman and two children endeavoring to escape, and the Indians pursued and took both the children. One of the men fired at the Indians, and saw one of them fall, when one of the girls he had possession of made her escape from him, but the other they took away. The Indian that was fired at ... cried out very much, but in a short time he got up and made off."

Horsfield found Holder's account credible, wrote it down, and passed it along to Governor William Denny. It illustrates a significant point: Many homesteaders had lacked firearms when Indian war parties first

Timothy Horsfield, painted by Valentine Haidt. Historical Society of Western Pennsylvania.

struck the Pennsylvania frontier settlements in October 1755. A year later, however, settlers who remained on their land had acquired guns and ammunition and had learned how to use them. This helped them resist the terrorist tactics employed by Indian raiders.

The settlers also relied heavily on companies of rangers who patrolled the roads and paths along the Blue Mountain. Assigned by top-ranking officers of the

Pennsylvania Regiment, these rangers were garrisoned at log stockades or other outposts located at strategic mountain passes and along important forest trails and roads.

One of the rangers was Lieutenant Jacob Wetterholt, who commanded a ranger company based at Everett's Fort near present-day Lynnport in Lehigh County. In midafternoon on July 9, 1757, a man hurriedly rode into the post with news that Indians had attacked a houseful of people eating dinner at the farm of Adam Clause about four miles away.

"I went immediately to the place with seven men besides myself and saw the murder, but the Indians was gone," Wetterholt said.

A number of neighbors had been helping Clause harvest his corn. "As they was eating their dinner, they were fell on by a party of savages," Wetterholt wrote later in his report. "Five of the whites took to their heels—two men, two women, and one girl—and got safe out of their hands." But twelve others—six adults and six children—had been killed. Nearly all the dead had been scalped. Also, a woman "was scalped and is yet alive, but badly wounded, one shot through the side and the other in the thigh."

Although the war party had a considerable head start, Wetterholt and his men gave chase. The rangers pursued the hostiles for about four miles and caught up with them in a thick grove of trees. They counted nine warriors.

One Indian sprang from behind a tree and took aim at Wetterholt, but the lieutenant rushed the man and spoiled the shot. A second warrior fired at the lieutenant, but the gun misfired, "and then both took to their heels, and I shot one ... through the body." The man fell on his face. Wetterholt reloaded his gun and took aim at an Indian who was leading a horse. Meanwhile, the wounded Indian "got up and run away, and I fired one (at) the other, and I think I shot him in ye buttocks, and my soldiers had opportunity to shoot three times, and then they (the Indians) got out of our sight in the thick groves, and we could not find them no more."

Later in the day the lieutenant sent a report of the raid and his response to Major William Parsons at Easton, about thirty miles to the east. He said that in their haste to get away, the Indians had left a good deal of plunder behind. "I got from them one mare and two saddles, one bridle and halter, and one bag with a keg of still liquor in it, and clothes and one brass kettle and four Indian cakes baked in the ashes of wheat meal."

Wetterholt also informed the major that several new soldiers in his company needed firearms, gun powder, and lead, "and I have sent this express to you hoping that you would help me with arms and ammunition."

Swollen, Icy Susquehanna Afforded Risky Passage for Indians, Soldiers

December 1756

The soldiers who built Fort Augusta during the summer of 1756 knew the Susquehanna River was prone to flooding, so they fortified the highest section on river bank just east of the confluence of the North and West Branches.

But nobody knew whether ice jams occurring on the river below the fort would flood it during the winter. Throughout the severe winter of 1756-1757, Major James Burd kept detailed notes on his nearly daily observations on both weather and river conditions.

Despite a heavy snowfall on December 16, Burd sent one hundred soldiers led by Captain David Jamison from Lancaster County down to Hunter's Fort, north of present-day Harrisburg, for provisions. Some men led pack horses down the riverside trail. Others sailed downriver in flat-bottom boats called bateaux.

When they reached McKee's Meadows, about twenty miles south of Fort Augusta, the boatmen found "that the river was so shut up (with ice) that they could proceed no further with the bateaux and had hauled them up upon the bank," Burd wrote.

The soldiers had enlisted to fight Indians, but throughout the winter they spent much time shoveling snow. On December 18, for instance, Burd said that he "employed all the soldiers in cleaning the snow out of the fort."

By December 19 at Fort Augusta, "the river full of ice," Burd wrote. "The West Branch shut up; it's left off

41

snowing. The North Branch open as yet, but very full of ice."

"Snowed all last night," Burd wrote on December 23. "Compute the snow this morning to be two foot, four inches deep."

The bitter weather persisted through January.

On January 23 soldiers coming up from Harris's Ferry brought two Conestoga Indians—William Sack and Indian Peter—to the fort. The Indians were en route to the Ohio River Valley as official messengers for the Pennsylvania colony.

Burd reported on January 24 that he "gave the Indians their powder horns full of powder and bullets and swan shot in their pouches,what they said would be sufficient for their journey. They required mocassins of me, and I told them I had not. They said they were barefooted, and ... I gave Indian Peter a pair of new shoes out of the Province store, and got a pair of new soles upon William Sack's shoes. With this provision they seemed satisfied. I likewise prepared hard biscuit for their journey ... and meat and every necessary fit for their journey."

Burd's journal entries over a three-day period show that William Sack and Indian Peter weren't eager to leave.

January 25: "This morning it snowed hard and has snowed all last night. I inquired of the Indians if they intended to proceed on their journey, and they informed me that the weather would not permit."

January 26: "The two Indians demanded of me two matchcoats, two tomahawks, one deerskin for to make mocassins, and some (rifle) flints. I told them I had neither matchcoats nor deerskins, but gave them two tomahawks and some flints. I ordered a canoe to be launched this morning to carry the Indians over the river. I informed the Indians that the canoe was ready, and they told me they would not go away today, but would go tomorrow."

At noon on January 27 "William Sack and Indian Peter crossed the river in my canoe. Sent three men to put them over and bring the canoe back. At their setting off, I saluted them with three platoons of 12 men, three roughs (beatings) of all the drums, three huzzahs, and one great gun."

The weather in subsequent days proved less than ideal for travelers on foot. As Burd noted:

January 31: "It rained very hard all this day. ... The river rises and is full of ice. It freezes towards evening."

February 1: "It rained, hailed and snowed all day, and is so extreme cold that the soldiers was not able to work out of doors."

February 3: "At 12 o'clock today heard two guns fired over the river. Looked out with the spyglass (and) ... discovered two Indians ..." They were on the west shore, opposite the fort, at the ravine that carries present-day County Line Road up Blue Hill.

"The Indians hung out a red hanker(chief), which I gave William Sack and Indian Peter for a signal ... I have sent a canoe and three men over for them, but the river is so full of ice driving in large cakes that I am afraid I can't get them brought over."

But the canoe managed to bring the Indians to the fort despite the icy conditions. "They report that the weather was so exceeding bad they could not travel, and the creeks and rivers impassable," Burd said. "The snow was so deep they could not walk, and therefore were forced to return."

Six days later, the conditions had improved to the point that the two Indians left Fort Augusta and headed downriver to the Conestoga Indian town near Lancaster. Burd sent three soldiers along as an escort. "They set out from this (fort) at 5 p.m.," Burd wrote. "This evening it rains and blows prodigiously."

Captain's Journal Documents Excitement, Dullness of Frontier Life

December 1756

As Benjamin Franklin had required, Captain John Van Etten kept a journal of daily life at Hyndshaw's Fort and recorded the experiences that his rangers had while on patrol. The entries span an eight-month period—from December 1, 1756, through July 22, 1757—and provide a comprehensive look at the activities, and sometimes forced inactivities, of Pennsylvania troops tasked with guarding the frontier against hostile Indians.

The captain often sent his men into the forest near the fort to gather firewood, which they used for both heating and cooking. Some soldiers stood guard while others cut and carried the fuel. At other times, he assigned them to sentry duty and occasionally accompanied them when he sent them out on patrol. Invariably, these were foot patrols.

Journal entries for these months give a flavor of conditions in the Minisinks:

December 1: "I went on scout with the oldest sergeant to see if there were Indians ..., but discovered none. We returned safe to the fort."

December 7: "I went on scout with two men and made no discovery; returned safe to the fort at night and found all in good order."

December 12. "Sunday and rainy, we all stayed at the garrison."

On December 14 the captain sent two men to guard a farmer named Jacob Swortwood who had grain that needed threshing in storage at his homestead, which was about four miles away from the fort. The next day, since the farmer hadn't finished the threshing, Van Etten again sent the guards to the Swortwood farm. The captain himself went out on a scout with four other men. "At night, when I returned, (Swortwood) told me that before he and said guard came to the field, they saw a small stack of rye set out in a large shock of thirty sheaves on a side, and places left in the middle to shoot out (of), and a bee hive set on the top," Van Etten said.

This structure was obviously a blind, and its presence raised suspicions that hostiles might use it to ambush unwary farm workers. On December 16 the captain took "six men to the place, and ordered two men with the wagons to come sometime after when I had surrounded the field, then to come and take their loads which was done, but no discovery made of the enemy. I went then with two men through the woods, and the rest of the men guarded the wagon, and we all returned safe to the fort."

December 17: "It snowed. I made a pair of moccasins for myself to scout in."

Winter brought a time of inactivity for Van Etten's rangers, and weather conditions became a frequent topic of journal entries.

By December 18 the snow had either stopped or tapered off, because the captain reported, "I went on scout with six men, and went about six miles from the fort and found the snow in many places half (a) leg deep. We discovering no enemy, all returned safe to the fort."

December 20: "It snowed, therefore we all kept the fort."

By December 21, the snow was knee-deep in the woods, and over the next several days the captain had the men remove snow from inside the fort. The captain's final entry for December came on the twenty-fourth. "And to the end of the month, the snow rendering it unfit for work or scouting, we cleared the parade and kept the men to their exercise twice a day," Van Etten wrote.

During the next several weeks, the soldiers went out on patrol only occasionally. Although sporadic attacks occurred elsewhere along the frontier, no hostiles were spotted near Hyndshaw's Fort. Van Etten reasoned that the forests around his fort were safe enough for his men to venture out in quest of firewood. After all, the supply of wood that they had gathered in December had begun to dwindle.

On January 8 he wrote, "Hauled firewood, having the advantage of the snow." Did this entry mean that the snow cover was deep enough for the men to use a horse-drawn sled?

The captain's entry for January 23 is a significant one: "Received order(s) ... that as soon as the season would admit, to discipline the men in the English exercise (of drilling with firearms), and to teach them the Indian method of war, ... which was immediately observed and daily practiced."

Months passed, and the occasional patrols that Van Etten sent out along the forest roads invariably returned to Hyndshaw's Fort without seeing signs of hostiles. Nor were any Indian-related incidents reported in the neighborhood. The soldiers, of course, knew that when winter ended, Indian raids would likely resume. But March passed quietly, and so did the early weeks of April. Then, just before sunset on Wednesday, April 20, Indians attacked near Fort Hamilton. A seventeen-year-old boy, Andreas Gundry-man, had been collecting firewood about a quarter mile from the fort when Indians suddenly appeared. They shot at him, but missed. The boy started running toward the fort, and soldiers heard him hollering for help. The Indians chased him, caught him, and killed him with their tomahawks. His lifeless body had been scalped by the time the soldiers reached him. The Indians, of course, were gone.

By coincidence, Van Etten had been at Fort Hamilton only a short time prior to the murder "and found all things in good order." The officer in command at Hamilton sent "an express ... to me at

Fort Hyndshaw" with news of the murder, the captain wrote in his journal.

April 21: "Went to Fort Hamilton with seven men." The youth had been "killed and scalped by the Indians, about one hundred rods (sixteen hundred feet) from Fort Hamilton." After the boy was buried, Van Etten "returned safe with my men to Fort Hyndshaw."

The Indians struck again four days later. Van Etten had sent Sergeant Leonard Dean and two men down to Samuel Dupui's fortified house for provisions on April 25. They were about two miles from their destination when gunfire erupted from along the road. The sergeant was mortally wounded, and the soldiers accompanying him fled.

As Van Etten recorded: "The two men returned and informed me of it, whereupon an alarm was beat, and the neighbors all gathered to the fort. Myself with seven men went off immediately and found him killed and scalped, and entirely stripped and shamefully cut, (so) that his bowels was spread on the ground."

The captain sent three men to Dupui's for a wagon, and "we carried him to said Dupui's, where we kept guard that night," the captain said. "Early in the morning we buried him in a Christian manner, and all returned to Fort Hyndshaw."

Due to reassignments of soldiers along the chain of forts, Van Etten's company was understaffed. Even so, on April 27, the captain decided it was time to be "increasing our sentinels as far as our weak circumstance would allow."

Around eight o'clock on the morning of May 5, "word came to me that an Indian was seen about three-quarters of a mile from the fort. I went out immediately in pursuit of them with eight men and one neighbor, and found it true by seeing his track, but could not come up with him," the captain said. But back at the fort, "my men ... saw him running from us at a considerable distance from us."

Later in the day Van Etten sent several soldiers to guard some neighboring farmers as they worked in a field. As one of the soldiers returned to the fort, the man "saw three Indians coming down a mountain near said field." The captain and three soldiers went out to investigate, but didn't encounter any Indians. "I stood on guard with two men, while one went to alarm the guard that was in the field," he said.

They returned to the post without incident, but that night some of the men on sentry duty noted "that the dogs kept an unusual barking and running to a particular place ..." On the morning of May 6, the soldiers ventured out to investigate "and found that an Indian had stood behind a tree about twenty-five yards from the fort. Being told, I went to see and found it true, his tracks being visible enough to be seen," the captain said. "In the afternoon I went on scout with four men and a neighbor, but made no discovery, and all returned safe to the fort."

Twelve days had passed since the sergeant had been killed, and on May 7 "I went with four men to a smith's shop where we made an instrument to take a bullet out of my horse, who was shot when Sergeant Dean was killed," the captain said. "All returned safe to the fort."

Repeated sightings of Indians had frightened the residents who lived in the area, and some decided to move into Hyndshaw's Fort until the danger passed. On Sunday, May 8 Van Etten reported that he and his troops "assisted some of the neighbors with their goods and families to the fort."

His men continued to make occasional patrols along the roads and trails near the fort. When Van Etten thought he could spare them, he sent soldiers to guard the farmers working in their fields.

On the morning of June 2, the captain sent five men to Dupui's for more provisions. In the afternoon the people at the fort were alarmed when they heard several gunshots. "I immediately, with three men, went to find out the reason, and found it to be some(one) who unwittingly shot at fowl in the river," the captain said. As for the men sent to Dupui's for supplies, "Our men all returned safe about sunset."

In late May Van Etten was summoned to Easton for a meeting with Major William Parsons, but the captain didn't make the forty-mile trip until mid-June. When the two officers finally met on June 14, Parsons provided him with ammunition—one hundred pounds of gunpowder, one hundred pounds of lead, and one hundred gun flints, but he also handed Van Etten a letter from Governor William Denny—"orders to remove to Fort Hamilton."

The captain left Easton in late afternoon and arrived at Fort Hamilton late the next day, which was twenty-five miles to the north. "Came safe to Fort Hamilton with the ammunition, about 6 o'clock (in the) afternoon, and found all things in good order," he wrote.

In the morning of June 16, he had the troops turn out for an inspection "and ordered them all to shoot at a mark" a distance away, the captain said. "Some of them did exceeding well."

Escorted by men from Fort Hamilton, Van Etten made the fifteen-mile trip to Hyndshaw's Fort without difficulty. "I immediately called the men to arms, and ordered everyone to get their clothes and whatever they had together as quick as possible, and be ready to march to Fort Hamilton," the captain said.

On June 19 at "about 9 o'clock in the morning we all marched from Fort Hyndshaw with all the baggage, and all arrived safe at Fort Hamilton, and met with no opposition," he wrote.

One of Van Etten's first tasks at Fort Hamilton on June 20 was to order a detail of six troops to Samuel Dupui's fort. Dupui's wife was ill, and Dupui had requested an escort of soldiers when he took his wife to see the doctor at Bethlehem about thirty-five miles to the south.

"The same day I went on scout with four men and one neighbor to get acquainted with the woods," Van

49

Etten said. But he also wanted "to see if any discovery could be made of the enemy." They found no signs of hostiles.

The next day the Dupuis stopped at Fort Hamilton on their way to Bethlehem, and the captain said he "ordered a guard of ten men, who went off under the care of a corporal." He also directed the men to go to Easton and deliver a message to Major Parsons. After that, they should return to Fort Hamilton as rapidly as possible.

Wednesday, June 22 passed quietly. As Van Etten remarked, "Nothing extraordinary happened, so all kept the fort." However, the events of Thursday, June 23 more than made up for the dullness of the prior day.

In late morning, five men who lived in the vicinity of Fort Hamilton went out to a pasture near Daniel Broadhead's house to get their horses. Indians suddenly fired on them and hit one, who went down. The other four escaped and, running to the fort, sounded the alarm. They told Van Etten "that one of them, John Tidd by name, was killed."

The soldiers who had escorted Samuel Dupui and his wife to Bethlehem had not yet returned, and the garrison was severely short-handed. Even so, the captain immediately selected nine men to go with him to investigate. This meant that only six soldiers remained in the fort. Before he left, Van Etten gave "strict orders to those left to fire the wall piece (most likely a swivel gun) to alarm us, if any attack should be attempted on the fort in my absence."

Van Etten's patrol headed out toward the site of the attack. As they hurried toward Broadhead's house, which was inside a stockade, they saw a small column of smoke arise from the back side. "Then traveling about a quarter of a mile in order to surround them, we heard four guns, the first of which being much louder than the rest," the captain said.

He interpreted the sound to mean that Fort Hamilton was being attacked, "whereupon we retreated back about a quarter of a mile, and hearing no more guns, my counsel was to go to the house, but my pilot, who was well acquainted with the woods, thought it best to place ourselves in ambush, for they would come that way," he said. "As we ascended the mountain in order to place ourselves, we saw the house in a blaze, and the pilot thought best to retire a little nearer between the house and the fort, where we might have a better view, and in the retreat we heard fourteen guns fired as quick after each other as one could count."

As the soldiers repositioned themselves, the men that were "nearest between the house and the fort soon saw twenty-seven (Indians) endeavoring to get between them and the fort. I, with the other party, saw five more coming on the other side. We found that we were discovered and like to be surrounded by a vast number, wherefore we all retreated and got between them and the fort."

Van Etten's men halted, and the warriors came into view. "I then challenged them to come, and fired at them ... Although at a considerable distance, it was generally thought one of them was killed, by their squatting and making off," the captain said. "Then we all retired to the fort."

As the soldiers returned to Fort Hamilton, "a scout of thirteen men from the Jersey ... came to the fort, being brought there by seeing the smoke and hearing the guns fired," he said.

The Jerseyans decided to pursue the war party, but first they accompanied Van Etten as he and his men went out to see whether John Tidd had actually been killed. "We found him killed and scalped, his body and face cut in an inhuman manner, cattle also lying dead on the ground, whereupon they (the Jersey men) all went off and left me with my small number to take care of the dead man. ... We took him up and returned to the fort."

It was at this time that the men who had escorted the Dupuis returned from Bethlehem and Easton.

51

The captain devoted much of June 24 to following up on events from the previous day. "I went with eighteen men and buried the man, then went from the grave in search and found fifteen cattle, horses and hogs dead, besides two that was shot, one with five bullets, the other with one," Van Etten said. "Yet there are many missing." He speculated that the Indians had taken some cows and a pig. In the evening, he sent two men to Easton with a report for Major Parsons.

On the morning of June 27 he sent eleven men "under the care of a corporal, with three neighbors, in search of some cattle, which they feared were taken or killed by the enemy." Later in the day, the soldiers returned and reported that they had found the livestock and that all were well.

The rash of Indian raids had prompted several nearby families to move into Fort Hamilton, if only temporarily, but this created a situation with complications all of its own. As Van Etten reported on July 6: "Complaint was made to me by some of the men that some of the neighbors which resided in the fort were lousy, by which means the whole garrison would soon be in the same condition. I then ordered the corporal with three men to assist him to make a search, and found that one Henry Gundryman and his family, and one John Hillman and his family were lousy."

The Gundrymans and Hillmans lived less than fifty yards from the fort, and Van Etten calculated that this distance was short enough that these neighbors could run to the fort in case of an alarm. "I ordered them out of the fort to their own house ... then employed the men to clean the fort within doors and without, which was accordingly done."

The next several weeks provided few signs of Indian war parties lurking in the woods, and the foot patrols that Van Etten sent out didn't encounter any hostiles. Then, on Tuesday, July 13, Van Etten himself made a curious discovery. With ten soldiers and three men from the neighborhood, "I went on scout, directing my course south about five miles from the fort, and from thence west two miles." He then charted a northerly course so that to return to Fort Hamilton, the patrol had to pass a meeting house where religious separatists held worship services. At the meeting house, "we found the enemy had lodged not long since, they leaving a bed of fern even in the pulpit," the captain said. But nobody saw any Indians and "all returned safe to the fort."

Van Etten made his last journal entry on Thursday, July 21. It appears that at around this time he resigned from the Pennsylvania Regiment, and that command of Fort Hamilton passed to Lieutenant Hyndshaw.

Hyndshaw's Fort was abandoned around this time. By autumn, the focus of the Pennsylvania Regiment had shifted farther west, and Fort Hamilton was also evacuated.

Friendly Indians Repeatedly Warn of French Attack on Fort Augusta

January 1757

In late January 1757 soldiers from Fort Augusta took two Indians across the icy Susquehanna River in a canoe so they could walk to the Ohio River Valley on official, but secret, business for the British colonies. But the weather was so severe that the Indians—William Sack and Indian Peter—returned to the fort after a few days and said they couldn't proceed.

This happened during the third year of the French and Indian War, and Pennsylvania officials were desperate for reliable information about French military activities along the Ohio and Allegheny Rivers. A well-used Indian trail along the West Branch led to a portage over the Allegheny Mountains to the Allegheny River in northwest Pennsylvania. Pro-French Indians often took this trail when they came east to raid in the vicinity of Fort Augusta, built in 1756 on land that is now part of Sunbury.

The fort's guns controlled the forks of the Susquehanna, but warriors loyal to the French often tried to ambush patrols and work parties sent out from the fort.

One snowy morning in late February 1757, for instance, Major James Burd, the commandant, sent soldiers with carts to bring several loads of stones back to the fort for use in a construction project. The major also sent a corporal named Barr with seven private soldiers to protect the work party.

Indians hiding in the woods shot at two sentries that the corporal had posted on a nearby hill. Barr ordered the rest of his men to return fire, but their guns wouldn't fire because their powder was wet. The men ran off, hurrying to the safety of the fort, and the warriors killed and scalped the sentries.

"Upon hearing the firing," Burd wrote in his journal, "I detached off Ensigns Broadhead and Allison with a party of twenty men to support the covering party ... Upon Mr. Broadhead's approach ..., the Indians from the slope of the mountain gave a general huzzah. ... The great shouts made me think their numbers were considerable. I immediately detached Captain Trump with an additional party of twenty men and two sergeants with orders to oblige them to fight or to pursue them and try to surround them." But the hostiles got away. As for the soldiers who had fled when the shooting started, Burd said: "I find these five ... ran off in disobedience to the corporal's orders, which was to advance upon the enemy and sustain the sentinels. I have confined them for cowardice."

On March 10 "At noon, came down from the North Branch in a canoe with English colors flying, five Indians, one named Nathaniel, and four more; they showed me Governor (William) Denny's passport, and told me ... ninety Indians more would be down here tomorrow or next day," the major wrote in his journal.

Two days later, Nathaniel gave Burd news from the French fort at modern Pittsburgh. "Nathaniel informed me that he saw his brother at Tioga (present-day Athens, Pa.), who told him he was just come from Fort DuQuesne, and before he left that place that six Frenchmen and three Indians had set out ... to come and view the works at Fort Augusta."

The ninety Indians eventually arrived at the fort in a fleet of fifteen canoes and three flat-bottom boats. They represented six upriver tribes: the Cayugas, Oneidas, Tuscaroras, Onondagas, Delawares, and Nanticokes.

They met with Burd in a formal council on March 18 "and informed me that there was eight hundred French and Indians marched from Fort DuQuesne against this fort, and they were actually arrived at the

Joseph Shippen

head of the West Branch of this river, and were there making canoes and would come down as soon as they were made, and desired me to believe this for truth, to be upon my guard, and to fight as long as I had one man alive.

"I gave them for answer that I was very much obliged to them for this piece of intelligence, that I was ready to receive the enemy, and that they might depend I would follow their advice," Burd said.

Captain Joseph Shippen, Burd's subordinate and brother-in-law, apparently was present when the friendly Iroquois gave this information to Burd. "They are all confident that this piece of news is true," Shippen said in a letter written that day.

Fort Augusta was designed to house a garrison of four hundred, but the number of soldiers present and ready for combat was frequently much lower, a fact that Burd tried to hide from visiting Indians.

In March 1757 the garrison was far below strength. As Shippen said, "We shall ... prepare ourselves in the best manner we can to give them a proper reception, though I am sorry to say we have at present on the spot but a hundred and ninety effective (soldiers) besides the sick and a party of thirty or forty men ... with the bateaux."

On March 21 another group of Indians "came down the river with English colors flying," Burd said. These Indians reported that they, too, knew about the force of French and Indians approaching Fort Augusta. "They would come down both branches of the river at once," the visitors warned Burd.

Despite the gravity with which the Indians delivered the warnings, the French soldiers and their Indian allies didn't assault the outpost. Indeed, Fort Augusta was never attacked during the war, which lasted until 1763.

Indians Attack as Pennsylvania Soldiers Evacuate Fort Halifax

October 1757

Andrew Montour bluntly delivered the news to John Harris and other Susquehanna Valley settlers: hostile Indians allied with the French were camped along the Susquehanna River about thirty miles north of Harrisburg, with "a French fort to be begun at Shamokin (present-day Sunbury) in ten days ..."

That was in late October 1755. Seven months later, a newly formed battalion of Pennsylvania soldiers left Harris's Ferry and marched upriver, heading for the forks of the Susquehanna. They had orders to erect a fort along the east shore on high land overlooking the confluence of the North and West Branches.

Commanding the expedition was Colonel William Clapham, a professional soldier from New England. Clapham's column moved slowly. Most soldiers walked, and the regiment was accompanied by a fleet of twenty flat-bottom boats carrying cannons, barrels of gunpowder, salted meat, and other supplies.

The battalion encountered few enemy Indians, but frequently saw signs that hostile warriors were tracking their progress.

About twenty miles north of Harris's Ferry, the colonel decided to build Fort Halifax—a square structure with log sides about 160 feet long and bastions at the corners—on the river bank just below Armstrong Creek. There was a saw mill along the creek, and soldiers cut and squared logs from the surrounding pine forest.

Andrew Montour

The post served as a supply depot for goods being shipped north to Shamokin, about thirty-five miles upriver.

As Clapham prepared to leave Halifax on July 1 and continue up the river, he reported to Governor Robert Morris: "I shall leave a sergeant's party at Harris' consisting of twelve men, twenty-four at Hunter's Fort, twenty-four at McKee's store (present-day Dauphin), each under the command of an ensign; and Captain (Nathaniel) Miles, with thirty men, at Fort Halifax ... I have removed all the stores from Harris' and McKee's to this place ..."

Five days later the Pennsylvanians reached the forks of the Susquehanna and began building Fort Augusta, which became the largest fort that the colony built during the French and Indian War. The French never besieged it.

For the next year and a half Fort Halifax operated as a supply base for Fort Augusta. Although hostile Indians occasionally attacked soldiers coming from or going to Halifax, the fort itself wasn't ever attacked.

During the summer of 1757 the army abandoned Fort Hunter, a small post located immediately south of the Blue Mountain, where Fishing Creek empties into the Susquehanna. This move was unpopular with settlers below the mountains. They soon began pressing to have the troops stationed at Fort Halifax reassigned to Fort Hunter so the soldiers could not only ship supplies to Fort Augusta, but also defend the downriver settlements. "The defense of Halifax is of no advantage, but a garrison at Hunter's, under the command of an active officer, will be of great service. It will render the carriage of provisions and ammunition for the use of Augusta more easy and less expensive, and by encouraging the inhabitants to continue in their places, will prevent the weakening of the frontier settlements," the Reverend John Elder, a clergyman at Paxton (present-day Harrisburg), wrote to Richard Peters, a member of the Provincial Council in Philadelphia, on July 30.

On August 25 residents of the township of Paxtang petitioned Governor William Denny and members of the Provincial Council and requested that Denny assign soldiers to Fort Hunter "with strict orders to range the frontiers daily."

The post at Hunter's mill occupied the river bank on the river's east shore immediately below the place where Fishing Creek flowed into the Susquehanna. Its vantage point provided a clear view of the entire river.

Commissary James Young, who attended the session, had visited Fort Halifax on several occasions and had had ample opportunity to assess its strategic value. He told the governor that Halifax, which Colonel Clapham had erected on the Susquehanna's east shore, was located "in a bad situation, being built beyond two ranges of hills." Young reported there was "no station for bateaux parties, having no command of the channel, which runs close on the western shore." Even worse, there was "a large island between the channel and the fort so that numbers of the enemy may, even in the daytime, run down the river without being seen by that garrison."

As for Fort Hunter, Young said "that though the fort, or blockhouse, at Hunter's was not tenable, being hastily erected and not finished, yet the situation was the best upon the river for every service, as well as for the protection of the frontiers."

These arguments persuaded the governor to close Halifax and reopen Fort Hunter. Consequently, on October 17 the commander at Fort Halifax, Captain Patrick Work, ordered his soldiers to evacuate Halifax and march south to Fort Hunter. To do so, they had to cross Peters Mountain.

As Work reported: "The advance guard, consisting of a sergeant and 12 men, as soon as they came to the top of the mountain discovered a party of Indians, I suppose about thirty in number. Our party advanced supposing them to be friends until they came within about a hundred yards, when the Indians fired upon them, which (fire) was returned briskly by our men."

Coming up with the main body of soldiers, the captain was still climbing the mountain when the shooting started. "I ... advanced with all speed, and when (I) joined the advance party, ordered them immediately to run up to the enemy, which they did very gallantly."

Work's troops wounded one Indian, "which we tracked some distance by the blood," but this man got away. The hostiles retreated so quickly that they "left five horses, which they had loaded with sundries taken from the inhabitants, which we got and I returned to the people" who owned them.

The officer expressed frustration about fighting Indians met in the woods: "We daren't fire on them till we ask whether they are friends, which gives them the advantage of the first fire, though we had not any killed or wounded."

When Governor Denny agreed to return troops to Fort Hunter, residents in the region promised to help the soldiers erect a log stockade around Fort Hunter. In February 1758, when Young inspected the chain of Pennsylvania forts between the Susquehanna and Delaware Rivers, he reported that Fort Hunter remained without a stockade. The commanding officer was Captain James Patterson, and Young said that he "ordered him (Patterson) to apply to the country to assist him to stockade the fort agreeable to their promise to His Honor the Governor."

Five months later Fort Hunter still lacked a stockade. Writing to Governor Denny from Carlisle on July 7, 1758, a British military engineer, Richard Dudgeon, reported that General John Forbes had ordered him to assess the defenses of Fort Hunter. "I have been to inspect the state of Fort Hunter, and am of opinion that stockading of it, and opening and deepening the ditch, according to the scheme left with the commanding officer there, will be sufficient to protect it against any Indian attack." The engineer added that the general had ordered the commanding officer at Fort Hunter "to see the work executed, by employing the country people, but ... it's apprehended he may meet with difficulties in calling in this assistance."

Ensign George Price became the commander at Fort Hunter a little later in the year. On July 22 Price reported to the governor that although "the stockades are cut," work had not yet begun to install them around the blockhouse. To erect the stockade, "I was to get the country people; and accordingly applied to the several justices of the peace for the townships of Paxton and Donegal, which latter I never had any answer from." However, "Parson Elder" of Paxton had informed him "that till harvest be over, the country people can do nothing." The ensign ended his letter by saying, "should the work of the fort be postponed till harvest be over, 'twill be yet three weeks before they begin."

Was the stockade ever built at Fort Hunter? Pennsylvania's historical record seems to be silent on this point. For many years, a riverfront park owned by Dauphin County has included the site of the fort. Although archaeologists have conducted a number of excavations at a spot on the bluff where the fort likely stood, physical evidence of a stockade has yet to be found.

Heated Dispute Embroils French Officer, Delaware Chief

1758

Rarely do historical records from the 1700s depict Indian leaders as articulate, quick witted, and even eloquent. When kept at all, the records of conversations between Native Americans and Europeans were invariably kept by white people, often government clerks or military aides, who tended to focus on the remarks of the whites and downplayed the comments of the natives.

The story that Teedyuscung, a colorful and controversial Delaware chief, told of a 1758 dispute between a French officer and two Delaware Indians at Fort DuQuesne stands out as an exception. He related the account to representatives of Governor William Denny, who wanted to end the Indian raids on the colony's frontier.

Although Teedyuscung's narrative constitutes high-grade hearsay more than anything else, it shows how news spread across the wilderness by word of mouth. It also illustrates how the loyalties of Indians allied with the French military in the Ohio River Valley began to waver when they realized that a British army was on its way to the Ohio Country from Pennsylvania.

In June 1758 Denny's agents—Charles Thomson and Christian Frederic Post—traveled to Fort Allen along the Lehigh River with instructions to go on to the Wyoming Valley along the North Branch of the Susquehanna River. They carried diplomatic messages intended for the Indians at Wyoming (present-day Wilkes-Barre), but Teedyuscung barred their way. There were pro-French war parties on the move, he told them, and this made the road to Wyoming too dangerous for white travelers.

Post and Thomson argued with Teedyuscung; they pointed out "that it was the custom of all (Indian) nations to suffer messengers of peace to go backwards and forwards, safe and unmolested; that unless this was practiced, two nations once at war could never be at peace again."

The chief agreed with this—"that what we said was right, but that the Six Nations, not him, had blocked up this road; that two hundred of them had gone to war in different parties; that they had passed through several towns on the Susquehanna; that in these towns the Delawares endeavored ... to dissuade them from going to war against the English, but they would not hear them."

Teedyuscung explained that these warriors were "chiefly of the Seneca Nation, and from three towns that lay near the French" in present-day western New York.

It was at this point that Teedyuscung told Thomson and Post about two Delaware Indians who had recently gone out to Fort DuQuesne from the Susquehanna. "They had surprised two French men, and shot them at a small distance from the fort," Teedyuscung said. "One was killed dead on the spot, but the other escaped on horseback to the fort, where he no sooner entered than he fell down and died."

As Teedyuscung told it, immediately after the two Delawares killed the French soldiers, the commander at Fort DuQuesne "called the Senecas together and told them the Catawbas had struck him."

The Catawba Indians lived in the Carolina colonies, and the British had been urging them to come north and fight against the French and their Indian allies. Also, the Catawbas were traditional enemies of the Six Nations, to which the Senecas belonged.

Soon after this, Teedyuscung said, "another Indian from Fort Augusta, being out on a scout near the French fort, killed another Frenchman. The commander again called the chiefs of the Senecas together and told them the Catawbas had struck him again."

The officer's comment provoked one of the Seneca chiefs to challenge him. "Why do you say the Catawbas have struck you? It is not the Catawbas that have done this, but your children the Delawares."

Many of the Delawares had sided with the French, and the Seneca's remark angered the commander. He "sent for the two chiefs of the Delawares, Tessawhenand and Cutkassanecamen, and complained of them in harsh terms." The three men grew heated, and "Tessawhenand told the commander he behaved like an old woman, to make so much noise about three men, and not to consider how many he had made him (the Delaware) lose. But though the bones of so many of his men lay scattered up and down in the woods, and all through his means, yet he made no noise about it. The Frenchman never heard him complain."

When the French officer persisted, the Delaware chief rebuked him: "If he had anything on his mind, to speak out and not scold any more like a woman. The commander, who was now very angry, told him, if he did not punish the Delawares he should die. At this Tessawhenand started up and, taking the commander by the hand, said, 'Now you speak like a man. You say I shall die. But I do tell you, I will not die alone. You shall die also. The English are coming up, and as soon as they strike you on one side, I will strike you on the other.'"

Teedyuscung explained to Thomson and Post that he had heard this story from a western Delaware named Willameghihink, a war captain among the Ohio Delawares. Willameghihink had come to eastern Pennsylvania to determine for himself "whether they (the English) were willing to make a peace with all the Indians, as they had been informed."

According to Teedyuscung, Willameghihink—who was also known as George Hays—had added that "the two chiefs had ... ordered their people to separate from the French, and consulted together how to be revenged. They proposed two schemes, one of which they agreed to follow. One was to wait till the English came up, and then fall on the French. The other was to pretend a reconciliation, and having a party of men ready, to take an opportunity and rush into the fort and drive the French out and then burn the fort, and this they think they can easily do. But before they took any step of that sort, they thought it necessary to know the truth of the reports respecting the English."

Post and Thomson included Teedyuscung's narrative in the report that they submitted to Governor Denny on June 16, 1758.

A British army commanded by General John Forbes marched across Pennsylvania during the summer and autumn of 1758. With English and colonial troops approaching, the French abandoned Fort DuQuesne in November 1758. During the next several months, many Delaware Indians came to the newly constructed Fort Pitt, made peace with the British, and began to trade with them. Present-day Pittsburgh grew up around Fort Pitt.

Moses Tatamy Travels 450 miles, Nearly Drowns to Bring about Peace

1758

As the Indian war wound down in Pennsylvania in mid-1758, war parties continued to cross the Delaware River and raid settlements in northern New Jersey. Between May 1757 and June 1758, twenty-seven New Jerseyans died in Indian attacks on the West Jersey side of the Delaware, according to the 1844 history of New Jersey written by John Barber and Henry Howe.

The New Jersey colonial government had allocated money for Governor Francis Bernard to pay Indians for settling old land claims. Eager to end the fighting, Bernard sent a Pennsylvania Indian, Moses Tatamy, into the upper Susquehanna River Valley with an invitation to a treaty that Bernard planned to hold in Burlington, N.J., later in the summer. A Delaware Indian, Tatamy was an experienced messenger and interpreter who was highly regarded by native leaders as well as colonial officials.

The timing for Bernard's initiative was good. Returning from a diplomatic errand for Pennsylvania Governor William Denny, messengers Charles Thomson and Frederick Post reported in mid-June that many enemy Indians were headed toward the Minisinks. They related a conversation they had had with a Munsee captain named Kelhapugh: "He said that several of the Munsees ... had been dispossessed of large tracts of lands in the Jerseys, without even receiving any consideration for them."

As if on cue, Samuel Dupui, an influential settler in the Poconos, reported that on June 14 "the Indians stole a ferry boat at a place called Wallpack and brought from the Jersey shore to this side a large number of Indians, as appeared by their tracks on the sand banks, so that we are in continual fear of their approach ..." Dupui had reason for concern. His homestead overlooked the Pennsylvania side of the Delaware at present-day Shawnee-on-Delaware.

Governor Bernard lost little time in getting his plan in motion. Traveling on foot, Tatamy left Philadelphia on June 27. By July 1, he and his two traveling companions, Indians who used the English names of David and Jonathan, had reached Tunkhannock about one hundred miles north of Bethlehem. "This is an old town. Nobody lives there, but over the river we saw some Minisink Indians, hunters, who called to us, and when we went over treated us kindly and gave us some bear meat and venison," Tatamy said later in his report. "The road this day broken and hilly."

They traveled all day on July 2, and Tatamy said that about an hour before sunset they encountered a company of fifty warriors who were returning from raids in the Minisinks:

They had with them four prisoners and three scalps. They said they had one chief man whom they called their father killed in a skirmish, and three wounded, of which one died by the way. The party consisted all of Senecas, but one of them talked Shawnee, and David understood that language.

At first they seemed to think us spies, and we were afraid of them, However, after talking with them we thought it best not to go past for fear they should take it ill, so we kindled a fire and sat down, then they came and sat with us and seemed pleased, but they told us some Delawares had pursued them and shot at them, and if the Delawares would do so again, they would either take them or kill them.

We told them where we came from, and where we were going, and our business. This satisfied them that we were not enemies. They told us that they had been in two companies, and that each company had taken a fort. They complained of the Delawares for having first

69

begun the war, and now sitting still when they, their uncles, had begun to make war on the English, and they said they would not sit still as they had done having once begun.

We saw one of the prisoners, a child between eight and ten years old.

The next day, which was Monday, July 3, the three men reached Tioga (present-day Athens) "where in wading the river, Moses Tatamy was almost drowned. All the houses in this town are in ruins, no Indians live there."

At Tioga, the Chemung River joined the Susquehanna, and a hard day's travel up the Chemung on July 4 got them to a Munsee village called Cobus Town. As they crossed the river flats to approach the village, they "traveled across some fine low land, thick settled, full of houses, fine corn fields. The people have plenty of meat, old corn, milk and butter," Tatamy said later. In the town itself, there were "three large houses and about ten small ones—about a hundred people, men women and children. Here we saw a white woman at a distance in a corn field."

They spent the night in Cobus's house. In the morning Cobus, whom Tatamy described as a Delaware Indian, accompanied them as they headed out to meet the head man. "We saw a great many houses and fine corn fields, spoke to a white boy, then crossed the river again and traveled about five miles to the king's house, all the way thick settled," Tatamy reported.

"At the king's house we stopped in a place provided for us till the other great men could be sent for," Tatamy said. "In this house live Alamewhehum, an old man, and Anandamoakin, a fat man, well dressed in French clothes, as are almost all the warriors. The old man is a friend of the English, and all who would be friends of the English hold with him, but the fat man is for the French, and, as we afterwards learned, is going soon to pay them a visit.

"About 12 o'clock the chief men came altogether, and we delivered our messages to them," Tatamy said. "While we were delivering them, all the rest seemed much pleased. ... But the fat man hung down his head and made no answer, or very little. After we had delivered the message, they all went out and entered into a consultation."

In effect, Tatamy had asked the Munsees to make a 225 mile journey to Burlington to discuss old land issues with Governor Bernard. A successful resolution of the old controversies over the land claims would likely bring an end to Munsee raids in northern New Jersey.

While the Indians conferred, Tatamy and his companions were invited to the house of Wenewalikas, which was a short distance away. "In the afternoon they sent for us again, and Moses Tatamy told them the message over again, at which they seemed to understand it much better."

That night a young man sought out Tatamy, gave him three strings of white wampum, and asked Tatamy to tell the New Jersey governor that "we are but a women nation and can do nothing of our selves till we have acquainted our uncles the Senecas, but we will send a man tomorrow to them to know what we shall do."

The man was saying that the Munsee people had become subservient to the Senecas and consequently lacked the authority to decide for themselves whether to accept Bernard's invitation. The Senecas would decide for them.

During the two meetings, Tatamy had presented the chiefs with wampum belts that corresponded to significant parts of his messages, but he had not given them paper documents intended to serve as a pass when their delegates arrived at Fort Allen on their way to Burlington. Nor had he presented them with an English flag that they would need to show to any Pennsylvania soldiers that they might encounter along the way. Tatamy and his companions discussed this issue before they went to bed for the night. "We were afraid if we gave them they would show them to the French. We concluded to keep them longer and went to sleep," he said.

During the morning of July 6, two young men came to visit the messengers. They were the sons of old friends who had moved from the Delaware Valley to the Susquehanna. The young men reported that they had recently traveled to the Allegheny River Valley and had visited the French fort at Venango (present-day Franklin). The French were running short of provisions, and French soldiers and Indian allies were receiving a daily ration of only "one pint of peas and one quarter of a pound of pork a day."

They told how a force of two hundred Indians had come "from beyond the (Great) Lakes to go down to Fort DuQuesne," but when they reached the fort, they learned that the food supplies there were nearly depleted. "The captain of the French fort gave them four quarts of beans to divide among them." Irate, "they shot a cow." This provoked the French officer, who demanded a share of the beef, but "they repulsed him and sent him back into the fort without any."

One of the men said that "some Indian spies" had been watching the English army as it marched west. The British soldiers were so numerous that the Indians "had been a whole day on one side of them, and intended to have gone round them, but they were so long a train they could not get round them that day."

Moses Tatamy remarked that "they need not try to get round them, for he supposed they reached to Philadelphia, as they had been going a great while, and were still loading wagons" there.

The young men reported that many of the Indians in the Ohio country "think the English will now beat the French, and they wish they may, but seem very fearful if they should, they will not be true to the Indians."

On the morning of July 7 the Munsee leaders again met in council and told Tatamy that they would send representatives to see the New Jersey governor. They also gave Tatamy three strings of black and white wampum and a belt with four rows of wampum. The wampum served to certify the council's remarks.

"We took out and delivered to them the letters and flag ... We told them they would be expected at Burlington in thirty days," Tatamy said. "They ... said they would be glad if Moses Tatamy would meet them at Fort Allen to be their interpreter as they came down through the inhabitants."

Tatamy and his companions left the Munsee town at about noon. They had acquired a canoe for the trip downriver, and a group of men accompanied them to the river to see them off. "Several times in conversation they said if the English were in earnest, why did they not send some of their own people with the messages? We told them that two white men were lately coming with messages, and had come as far as Nescopekun (Nescopeck), but were stopped by the Indians for fear the warriors would meet them and kill them," Tatamy said.

The travelers made good time going downriver. On the night of July 8, instead of camping along the way, they "let the canoe drive down all night, and in the morning stopped and breakfasted" at the village of Papunhank, a Munsee leader. Papunhank "was well pleased with our message, and said he would come down" to Burlington, Tatamy reported.

The travelers reached Bethlehem by July 12, and two days later Tatamy was in Philadelphia. His mission had taken eighteen days.

Governor Bernard convened the treaty at Burlington on August 7. A second treaty was held at Easton two months later. More than five hundred Indians attended, and the Munsees formally released all the lands they had claimed in New Jersey. The treaties represented major developments toward reestablishing peace between New Jersey colonists and the Munsee Indians.

British Military Engineer Wrote the Specs for Powder Magazine at Fort Augusta

May 1758

On July 9, 1755, after General Edward Braddock's British troops forded the Monongahela River for the second time, the advance guard began the final eight-mile leg of its march to Fort DuQuesne at present-day Pittsburgh.

A squad of carpenters walked in front of the soldiers in the vanguard, and in front of the carpenters went Lieutenant Harry Gordon, a military engineer charged with a special task. The army was following a narrow Indian path westward through the forest, and Gordon was responsible for marking the way for a road so that the carpenters could cut down trees and clear brush. That way, the army would have a road rather than a trail over which to march.

It was Gordon, moving well in advance of Braddock's main force, who first spotted French soldiers and Indian warriors running east along the path in order to stop Braddock's advance, according to Winthrop Sargent, in his 1856 classic book, *History of an Expedition against Fort DuQuesne*.

As the battle took shape, the Indians and French fought from behind trees and slew hundreds of the British regulars, whose officers forced them to form lines in clearings and to shoot at Indians and French troops they couldn't see. The fight has gone down in American history as Braddock's Defeat.

Three years passed before the British Army made another serious effort to evict the French from Fort DuQuesne, a stockade post they had built at the confluence of the Allegheny and Monongahela Rivers.

As General John Forbes gathered his army in southeastern Pennsylvania and prepared to head west, Harry Gordon, now a captain, was sent up the Susquehanna River to inspect Fort Augusta at present-day Sunbury to recommend improvements.

Gordon's report, dated May 6, 1758, recommends the construction of a subterranean powder magazine:

A magazine ought to be built in the south bastion, twelve by twenty foot in the clear. ... The wall of the magazine to be two and a half feet thick with three buttresses, two foot thick at the bottom, beveling to nine inches at top in each side. The breadth of the buttresses, three and a half feet,

The magazine to have an arch of two and a half brick thick and to be underground within one and a half foot of the top of the arch.

The walls seven foot high from the level of the floor, and to have a foundation two foot below the floor.

Great care taken to lay the joists, and to fill up between with rubble stone and gravel, rammed; the joists to be covered with plank two and a half inch thick. An air hole one foot square to be practiced in the gravel end, opposite the door.

The passage to the magazine to have a zig-zag, and over the arch some fine plaster laid, then covered with fine gravel and four foot of earth atop.

Gordon also listed "ammunition and stores wanted at Fort Augusta." These included:

- Sixteen pieces of cannon, four of which twelve or nine pounders, the rest six;
- Fifty rounds of shot for each gun;
- Eight rounds of grape shot; and
- Twenty-four barrels of powder for cannon.

Much of the original Fort Augusta was demolished long ago, but the powder magazine survives, and visitors to Hunter House, the headquarters of the Northumberland County Historical Society in Sunbury, can see it. A fence surrounds it so visitors can't descend the stairs to peer inside.

REMAINS OF THE OLD MAGAZINE OF FORT AUGUSTA.

Arguably, the magazine is Northumberland County's oldest surviving structure. What's more, Harry Gordon's written recommendation provides solid documentation for the date of its construction.

Not only did Gordon take part in Forbes's campaign that in late 1758 forced the French to abandon Fort DuQuesne at present-day Pittsburgh, but the engineer also designed Fort Pitt, the defense that Forbes built as the main British outpost on the Ohio River.

Posse from Lancaster Stumbles into a Gunfight at Muncy Hill

Summer 1763

During the summer of 1763 Indian war parties came down the Susquehanna River's West Branch, slipped past Fort Augusta at present-day Sunbury, and raided downriver settlements in Cumberland and Lancaster Counties.

That August, "a party of volunteers from Lancaster county, one hundred and ten in number," organized, armed, and marched up the Susquehanna, reported I. Daniel Rupp in his 1844 book, *History of Lancaster County.* They planned to destroy a Native American town situated on an island in the West Branch near either present-day Jersey Shore or Lock Haven. They suspected that most of the attacks were being committed by Munsee warriors living in this town.

When the vigilantes from Lancaster County got to Fort Augusta, "we sent a man forward to see whether Andrew Montour was there, but he was not."

This quotation comes from an 1811 book compiled by Archibald Loudon and titled, *A Selection of Some of the Most Interesting Narratives of Outrages Committed by the Indians in Their Wars with the White People.* Loudon didn't identify the man who wrote about the expedition, but assured his readers that it came "from one of the men who was at the Battle of Muncy, on whose veracity we can depend."

By 1763 Andrew Montour was well-known on the Pennsylvania frontier. Part French and part Indian, he had spent many years in the Susquehanna River Valley. Often he had worked as an interpreter for English colonial officials in their dealings with Indian

78

Indians attacking a cabin

leaders, but he had also distinguished himself both as a warrior and a guide.

By 1763 Montour was living about five miles northwest of present-day Northumberland—on the river flats near where the Chillisquaque Creek flows into the West Branch.

79

The Lancaster men seemed to know a lot about him. As Loudon's source reported: "We had apprehended that Montour knew of our coming and had gone to inform the Indians at the town called Great Island, or Munsee town, but when we got to the fort, the officers ... wanted to persuade us not to go over, as the Munsee Indians were friendly to the white people."

The Munsees were part of the Delaware Tribe, and the Lycoming County community of Muncy is named for them.

The vigilantes rejected the soldiers' advice and started up the West Branch. Apparently on foot, they followed an Indian trail known as the Great Shamokin Path. It went from Sunbury through the present-day towns of Northumberland, Milton, Watsontown, Montoursville, and Williamsport.

They hadn't gone very far when they "saw Montour coming down in a canoe with a hog and some corn which he had brought from his plantation," the source reported. "When he came near, we called to him, upon which he landed and enquired our business. We told him, and asked his advice whether it was proper to proceed or not. He said they were bad Indians, and that we might use them as we pleased."

That night, the Lancaster men camped at Montour's farm. In the morning, they crossed the Muncy Hill where they "discovered fires where the Indians lay the night before. Here we consulted whether to proceed or not." One of the leaders, a man named William Patterson, decided to turn back, "and we all followed."

These men had come north looking for trouble, and as they withdrew, trouble suddenly found them. As the Lancaster men started south, they ascended the Muncy Hill where "we met with a party of Indians which we engaged, had two men killed, and four wounded, two of which died that night. We then went and secreted the dead bodies in a small stream to prevent their being discovered by the enemy. By that time it was night."

The unidentified man said that "about twelve of us ran up the hill where we heard them (the Indians) running but could not see them. We then came back to where they had fired on us at first, and found that the rest of our party were gone."

Unfamiliar with the landscape, they encountered three more of their comrades in the darkness, then made their way along a forest trail.

"In this path we traveled until daylight, when we saw a smoke, and ... saw some Indians sitting about a fire. I then turned to the right into the woods, and some of our men followed me and some went on in the path till the Indians saw them, and seized their guns. We then raised our guns to fire, but the Indians cried, 'Don't shoot, brothers! Don't shoot!'

"We answered, 'We will not if you do not!'"

Nobody fired, and the Lancaster men quickly realized that they outnumbered the three Indians, all men.

The Indians expressed surprise when "we told them we had an engagement the evening before with some of their people. They said it was impossible."

The Indians said that they themselves were returning from a frontier town where they had purchased some goods.

When the whites informed the Indians that they were taking them as captives, "the three Indians began to tremble, and, leaving the victuals they were preparing, proceeded with us."

George Allen was one of the Lancaster volunteers, and "after we had traveled a short distance, I asked George Allen what we should do with the prisoners. He said we would take them to the fort and deliver them up to the commander. I told him if we do that, perhaps they will let them go, or send them to Philadelphia ..."

At this point, the narrator told Allen that a few weeks earlier, Indians had killed five of his neighbors during a skirmish in the Juniata River Valley, "and I had hard running to save my own life."

He added, "I have declared revenge on the first Indian that I saw, and am glad that the opportunity now offers."

"Why," said Allen, "would you kill them yourself, for you can get no person here to help you."

"There is enough," replied the unidentified narrator, "that will help me to kill them."

"Where will you kill them?" Allen asked.

"I told him on the hill that is before us, which lies between the two branches of the Susquehanna River, near the North Branch.

"When we came to the top of the hill, the prisoners asked liberty to eat some victuals, which we allowed them. They directed us to where we might find it among their baggage. We went and found it, and gave it to them.

"While they were eating we concluded who would shoot at them. There was six of us willing to shoot, two men to each prisoner, and as soon as they were done eating, we told them to march on before us, and when they had gone about thirty yards, we fired at them and the three fell, but one of them ... was shot only through the arm, and fell with that arm uppermost and bloodied his body, which made us believe that he was shot through his body."

Loudon's writer said that after this Indian was scalped, one of the frontiersmen decided to remove a "good pair of leggings" from the corpse.

The man managed to remove the first legging, but before he could get the second one, "the Indian started up and ran. The man was surprised at his raising from the dead, and before he could get any assistance, he (the Indian) had made his escape."

The killings apparently occurred somewhere on Montour Ridge north of present-day Northumberland as the Lancaster men headed south toward Fort Augusta.

Legend Shrouds the Story of Regina Leininger, a Historical Figure

The story of Regina, the German child kidnapped by Indians early in the French and Indian War, is one of the most enduring and best-known accounts to emerge from Pennsylvania's frontier era.

Abducted when she was about twelve, the child grew up with the Indians in Western Pennsylvania and Ohio. Nine years later, a British army brought her and many other captives back to the European regions of Pennsylvania.

The newly freed captives were being processed at Carlisle, and her mother went there to look for her among the rescued prisoners. At first, mother and daughter failed to recognize each other, but Regina suddenly made the connection when the mother began singing a familiar hymn.

This powerful story is the stuff of legend, and there's ample historical documentation for its broad outline.

Israel D. Rupp, in his 1846 book, *Early History of Western Pennsylvania*, tells how Colonel Henry Bouquet, a Swiss soldier, led a British army against hostile Indians in Ohio in 1764. He forced the natives to return all the white prisoners they had taken since the war had begun a decade earlier.

Rupp's account is firmly based on historical fact. Bouquet's force—the 42nd Highlanders, Royal Americans, and two battalions of Pennsylvanians— marched out of Carlisle in August and took more than a month to reach Fort Pitt at Pittsburgh. At some point, soldiers from Maryland and Virginia joined the expedition.

By late October Bouquet's army reached the Forks of the Muskingum, about 120 miles west of Pittsburgh. The soldiers were deep in Indian country. When Bouquet met the chiefs, he demanded the release of all their captives. By the time he returned to Fort Pitt in late November, "he had forced the surrender from the Indians—Mingoes, Shawnees and Delawares—of 363 prisoners held in their towns," reported Edward G. Williams in writing about the campaign.

Many of these captives, especially the younger ones, had been adopted by native families. They had learned to dress and live in the manner of their new relatives, and had learned Indian languages. Also, more than a few of the youngest captives had forgotten the European languages that they had spoken as children.

Many native families had become emotionally attached to the captives they had adopted and were devastated when Bouquet forced the Indians to return them. As a Shawnee chief, Lawaugqua told Bouquet, "Father ... We have brought your flesh and blood to you. They have all been united to us by adoption, and although we now deliver them up to you, we will always look upon them as our relations."

When the colonel brought the prisoners to Carlisle, scores of settlers—especially those who had lost relatives during Indian raids—traveled to Carlisle to see if Bouquet had rescued members of their families. There's plenty of documentation for this as well.

However, the only place in the historical record where the Regina story appears is in the writing of a respected Lutheran clergyman of the eighteenth century, the Rev. Henry Melchior Muhlenberg.

According to the late C. Hale Sipe, a woman called at Muhlenberg's house in Philadelphia in February 1765 and told him a remarkable story. She said that Indians had kidnapped her two daughters in an October 16, 1755, raid on their Pennsylvania homestead. Nine years later, after Bouquet informed the public that he had brought many of the freed

Henry Melchior Muhlenberg

prisoners there, she went to Carlisle hoping to find her daughter.

Writing in *The Indian Wars of Pennsylvania*, Sipe said: "She went up and down the long line (of prisoners), but ... failed to recognized the little girls she had lost. Colonel Bouquet compassionately suggested that she do something which might recall the past to her children."

The mother began singing a German hymn, a line of which (in English) said, "Along yet not alone am I."

"She commenced singing, in German," Sipe said, "but had barely completed two lines when poor Regina rushed from the crowd, began to sing also, and threw her arms around her mother."

Muhlenberg's story quickly took root in Pennsylvania folklore, even though, as Sipe said, "Muhlenberg does not give the name of the family and does not definitely give the location of the tragedy."

In time, many nineteenth century historians concluded that the family's surname was Hartman and that the kidnapping took place near Orwigsburg in Schuylkill County.

However, Sipe said that later historians concluded that Regina was the daughter of Sebastian Leininger, who was killed during the Penns Creek raid on October 16, 1755, in present-day Union County. They agreed that Regina's mother was Sebastian's widow and that the Leininger farm was a little west of New Berlin.

Regina and her older sister Barbara were taken in the raid. Barbara later escaped and wrote a detailed narrative of her captivity.

There's a tombstone in a cemetery near the Berks County community of Stouchsburg with the following inscription: "Regina Leininger in legend Regina Hartman as a small child held Indian captive ..."

Susquehanna Soldiers Walk to Boston to Join the American Army

1775

The American Revolutionary War was just beginning when a company of soldiers trooped into Northumberland in late June 1775.

"About 12 o'clock marched into this town, from the Great Island, or Indian land, fifty miles up the river (at modern Lock Haven), thirty young fellows, all expert riflemen, with a drum and fife, under Captain Lowdon," wrote Philip Vickers Fithian, a young clergyman, in his journal entry for Wednesday, June 28.

Bound for Boston, they were walking to Massachusetts, where they intended to join the American Army. As they went, they were stopping in towns and villages along the way to recruit additional men.

The soldiers stopped in Northumberland, but only briefly. "They passed on ... soon to Sunbury, where they remained until Monday," Fithian wrote.

The clergyman recorded colorful details about life in the Susquehanna River Valley during the early months of the revolution. There were few churches and fewer clergymen in the region, and Fithian, who had been sent to preach at recently settled communities along the river's West Branch, found a prosperous valley whose inhabitants were eager for news of the war. Letters and newspapers arrived on horseback, carried from Philadelphia by postal riders who made the four- or five-day ride over the mountains.

As Fithian reported for Thursday, June 29:

"After dinner I went down the river ... in a small boat, for exercise and recreation. The river is perfectly transparent—so clear that you can see, in the deepest parts, the smallest fish.

"In the evening came the Philadelphia papers. All things look dark and unsettled. The Irish regiments have arrived. Government is strengthening its forces; the Americans are obstinate in their opposition. The Virginians have differed highly with their governor, and he has thought it necessary to go on board, with his family, of one of His Majesty's ships."

Fithian was a Presbyterian minister. There were Presbyterians living in Northumberland, but they hadn't yet built a church, so on Sunday, July 2, Fithian conducted worship services in the private residence of a Mr. McCartney. He preached twice and noted that several people attended both sermons. These included "Mrs. Hunter, Captain Hunter's lady, who lives on the other side of the water at Fort Augusta, and is burgess (lieutenant) for his county, and is ... down at Philadelphia."

The Hunters, he had learned, lived in a house "within the walls of Fort Augusta."

After service, Mrs. William Scull invited the preacher to coffee.

"While we were at coffee, the post came into town," Fithian wrote. "We have in the papers accounts of the Battle of Bunker Hill, near Boston, where the Provincials were worsted; accounts of General Washington and his aide-de-camp, Mr. Mifflin, leaving Philadelphia for the North American camp."

On Monday, July 3, the clergyman wrote:

"After dinner, Mr. (Rueben) Haines, the proprietor of the town, took me to see a lot he is about to give to the Presbyterian Society. It is a fine high spot on the Northway Street, and near the river; also near it is a fine spring of good water."

Present-day Priestley Avenue is approximately where Northway was.

Wednesday, July 19: "At the invitation of Mr. (William) Scull and Mr. (John) Barker I went, after dinner, over the river to Captain Hunter's. I was formally introduced by these gentlemen to him. He talks but little, yet with great authority. ... We drank with him one bowl of toddy and passed on to Sunbury.

"The town lies near a half mile below the fort, on the north side of the main branch. It may contain an hundred houses. All the buildings are of logs but Mr. Maclay's, which is of stone and large and elegant. ... Northumberland at the point has a good appearance from this town."

Maclay's stone structure still stands at the corner of Front and Arch Streets.

At Sunbury, Fithian reported, "the inhabitants were mustering arms—blood and death, how these go in a file!

"As we were returning in our slim canoes, I could not help thinking with myself how the savage tribes, while they were in possession of these enchanting wilds, have floated over this very spot."

Fithian noted that in late June the Continental Congress, which was meeting in Philadelphia, had called for the colonies to observe Thursday, July 20 "as a day of public humiliation, fasting and prayer." The idea quickly took hold in Northumberland, and in early July, several influential men in the village invited Fithian to give two sermons on that day.

Fithian's entry for Thursday, July 20 describes the event: "I rose by six; the town quiet. ... Stores shut and all business laid aside. By ten many were in town from the country. Half after eleven we began. I preached in Mr. Chatham's house, in the Northway Street. It is a new house, just covered, without partitions. It was thronged. Many were in the chamber; many in the cellar; many were without the house. ..."

As for the sermon itself, Fithian confided to his journal that "I spoke in great fear and dread. I was never before so nice an audience; I never spoke on so solemn a day. In spite of all my fortitude and practice, when I began my lips quivered; my flesh shrank; my hair rose up; my knees trembled. I was wholly confused until I had almost closed my sermon. Perhaps this feeling was caused by entirely fasting, as I had taken nothing. ... In the afternoon service felt much better, but was under the necessity of reading both sermons."

Note: It took two months for the riflemen that Fithian met in late June to make their way to Massachusetts. Required to furnish their own clothing and provide their own firearms, these men literally marched into history. One of them was Aaron Wright, who kept a journal. He reported that the company was sworn in in Northumberland on June 29 and remained at Sunbury "until the 7th of July, when we got orders to march ... The next morning we marched on board the boats," which took them down the Susquehanna to Harris's Ferry. On July 13, the soldiers "reached Reading, where we got our knapsacks, blankets, etcetera." It was early September when they arrived at Cambridge, across the harbor from Boston. There the outfit became part of the Second Regiment of the Army of the United Colonies, commanded by General George Washington. During the next several years, they fought at Boston, Long Island, Trenton, Princeton, and Saratoga; wintered at Valley Forge; and took part in the Sullivan Campaign against the Iroquois in 1779.

Militia Scout Escapes from Indian War Party, Returns to Fort Augusta

1777

Moses Van Campen earned a reputation as a brave and colorful Indian fighter at a time when Iroquois warriors regularly terrorized the Susquehanna Valley. That was during the American Revolutionary War.

Born in New Jersey in 1757, Van Campen was the oldest of ten children. He grew up in the Delaware River Valley and moved with his parents to present-day Columbia County in the 1770s. He helped his family establish a farm along Fishing Creek.

When the revolution began, the young man joined the Pennsylvania militia and in 1777 served a three-month tour with Colonel John Kelly at the western-most settlements along the Susquehanna River's West Branch.

As Samuel Hazard reported in an 1833 edition of *Hazard's Register of Pennsylvania*, "In the spring of 1777 Van Campen took the command a small detachment of ... men, and built a small fort on the waters of Fishing Creek." This was Fort Wheeler.

Van Campen, who attained the rank of lieutenant by age twenty, had many dangerous exploits during the war. This is the story of one of them.

Late in the winter of 1779-1780, Van Campen took a break from soldiering and spent time with his family along Fishing Creek. He helped his father rebuild the farmhouse, which Indian raiders had burned. This was the time of year when settlers went into the woods and gathered syrup from the sugar maples. There a snow cover, and an Iroquois war party came looking for white settlers off their guard in the sugar camps.

Moses Van Campen

In the process, they killed and scalped Van Campen's father and brother and captured Van Campen and some others. It was March 29, 1780—just after the beginning of spring.

The warriors led their prisoners along the snow-covered trail that led north to the Finger Lakes of New York. Van Campen realized the Indians intended to take their prisoners to Fort Niagara, a British post located where the Niagara River flowed into Lake Ontario.

As they traveled, the warriors taunted the captives. They told the prisoners that they themselves wouldn't reach Fort Niagara, but that their scalps would. Before they got to the fort, "they should feel the tomahawk."

The previous September an American army led by Major General John Sullivan had marched up the Susquehanna and invaded the Iroquois homeland. The soldiers burned more than forty Iroquois towns and villages, destroyed the cornfields and orchards, and burned the granaries where the Iroquois had stored their harvest.

Van Campen had taken part in the Sullivan expedition, and he realized that the Iroquois would be especially cruel to any white prisoners brought into their region that spring. He decided that he and the two other prisoners needed to attempt an escape even though the Indians outnumbered them.

To quote *Hazard's Register*:

"On the night of the second of April, about 12 o'clock, the prisoners concluded that all the Indians were sound in sleep. Van Campen had previously procured a knife. They rose, cut themselves loose, and immediately removed all the (Indians') arms."

The warriors didn't stir, and the captives tomahawked and shot most of them. Van Campen, afterwards, said that only one Indian escaped.

Van Campen and his comrades scalped the dead Indians, then hurried off to the North Branch, "built a raft and set sail for Wyoming."

At Wilkes-Barre they obtained a canoe and came downriver. They reached Fort Jenkins, a Pennsylvania post along the river between modern Berwick and Bloomsburg, and learned that soldiers and settlers had all feared that Van Campen and the other prisoners had been killed.

After that, "I went to Sunbury. ... I was received with joy, my scalps were exhibited, the cannons (at Fort Augusta) were fired, etc."

In his old age, Van Campen included this story when he and his grandson, John N. Hubbard, wrote a book about the old soldier's experiences. Published in 1842, the book was titled, *Sketches of Border Adventures in the Life and Times of Moses Van Campen.*

Indian Attacks Terrify Susquehanna Settlers, Trigger Flight from Valley

1778

Long ago someone wrote a bit of information on a thin piece of paper and pasted the paper on the back of a very old platter, which was white with blue edging. The note has become brown with age, but most of the writing remains legible.

In part, the note says: "A few days before the Wyoming Massacre by the Indians on July 3rd and 4th, 1778, a friendly Indian took a family down the Susquehanna in a raft to safety. This platter was included in their dishes. ..."

Specific facts about the history of this particular

MASSACRE OF WYOMING.

Charles Weimar's "Massacre At Wyoming Valley"

platter are hard to come by, but there's plenty of background information available about central and northeastern Pennsylvania during this phase of the American Revolutionary War.

In the summer of 1778 Indians aligned with the British terrorized settlers living along both the North and West Branches of the Susquehanna River. Many people fled downriver to Fort Augusta at Sunbury, where Colonel Samuel Hunter commanded the soldiers protecting the region.

In early July 1778 a force of Indians and Loyalists attacked settlers from Connecticut who had moved into the Wyoming Valley on the North Branch. Afterwards, many Connecticut people descended the North Branch in a panic and brought word of the battle to Fort Augusta.

"Wyoming is totally abandoned," William Maclay wrote in a July 12, 1778, letter. He had just left Sunbury for present-day Harrisburg, then called Paxton.

Indians attacking a homestead

"I brought my family by water to this place," he wrote. "I never in my life saw such scenes of distress. The river and the roads leading down it were covered by men, women and children flying for their lives, many without any property at all."

Maclay said that people living in Northumberland and Sunbury became terrified when they heard the stories of the refugees from the Connecticut settlements: "The miserable example of the Wyoming people, who have come down absolutely naked among us, has operated strongly, and the cry has been, 'Let us move while we may and let us carry some of our effects along with us.'"

Pioneer families were also deserting the West Branch. One settler who fled was Juda Thomson, a New Jersey woman who in the early 1770s had come to the Susquehanna from Hunterdon County along with her husband John and small son. The family settled near the Loyalsock Creek in what has become Lycoming County.

In June 1778 Indians killed and scalped her

husband then burned the Thomson homestead. Juda and her son soon found themselves among the many refugees gathered at Fort Augusta. Eventually, mother and child walked back to New Jersey.

Flight along the West Branch was rampant. "I took my family safely to Sunbury, and came back in a keelboat to secure my furniture," scout Robert Covenhoven reported. "Just as I rounded a point above Derrstown, (present-day Lewisburg), I met a whole convoy from all the forts above. Such a sight I never saw in my life. Boats, canoes, hog troughs, rafts hastily made of dry sticks, every sort of floating article had been put in requisition and were crowded with women, children, and plunder. Whenever an obstruction occurred at any shoal or ripple, the women would leap out into the water and put their shoulders to the boat or raft and launch it again into deep water. The men of the settlement came down in single file, on each side of the river, to guard women and children."

The plight of the refugees was desperate. As Maclay reported, "Something in the way of charity ought to be done for the many miserable objects that crowd the banks of this river, especially those who fled from Wyoming."

The old white platter that came down the North Branch from Wyoming that summer survives in the collection of a southeastern Pennsylvania woman, who says she would like to know more about it. There are many questions: Did the platter ever reach Fort Augusta? Who were the people who brought it? What happened to them?

Selected Bibliography

Colonial Records. vol. VII. Harrisburg, PA: Theo. Fenn & Co., 1851.

Heckewelder, John Gottlieb Ernestus. *An Account of the History, Manners, and Customs of the Indian Nations, Who Once Inhabited Pennsylvania and the Neighboring States*. Philadelphia: Publication Fund of the Historical Society of Pennsylvania, 1876. (Reprint edition by Arno Press Inc., 1971)

Hunter, William A. *Forts of the Pennsylvania Frontier, 1753-1758*. Harrisburg: Pennsylvania Historical and Museum Commission, 1960.

Jennings, Francis. *Empire of Fortune: Crowns, Colonies and Tribes in the Seven Years's War in America*. New York: W.W. Norton and Company, 1988.

Loudon, Archibald. *A Selection of Some of the Most Interesting Narratives of Outrages Committed by the Indians in Their Wars with the White People. 1808-1811, Volumes I and II*. Carlisle, PA: The Press of A. Loudon, 1811. (Reprint edition by Garland Publishing Inc., 1977.)

Meginness, John F. *Otzinachson: A History of the West Branch Valley of the Susquehanna*. vol. 1, Williamsport, PA: Gazette and Bulletin Printing House, 1889.

Pennsylvania Archives, First Series. vols. I, II, and III. Edited by Samuel Hazard. Philadelphia: Joseph Severns & Co., 1853.

Rupp, I. Daniel. *History and Topography of Dauphin, Cumberland, Franklin, Bedford, Adams and Perry Counties*. Lancaster: Gilbert Hills, Proprietor & Publisher, 1846.

Rupp, I. Daniel. *History and Topography of Northumberland, Huntingdon, Mifflin, Centre, Union, Columbia, Juniata and Clinton Counties.* Lancaster: G. Hills, 1847.

Swift, Robert B. *The Mid-Appalachian Frontier: A Guide to Historic Sites of the French and Indian War.* Gettysburg, PA: Thomas Publications, 2001.

Wallace, Paul A.W. *Conrad Weiser, 1696-1760: Friend of Colonist and Mohawk.* Philadelphia: University of Pennsylvania Press, 1945.

Wallace, Paul A. W. *Indian Paths of Pennsylvania.* Harrisburg: Pennsylvania Historical and Museum Commission, 1971.

Wallace, Paul A.W. *Indians in Pennsylvania.* Harrisburg: Pennsylvania Historical and Museum Commission, 1970.

Made in the USA
Middletown, DE
25 June 2018